*The Art of Being
a Good Friend*

Hugh Black

The Art of Being a Good Friend

How to Bring Out the Best in
Your Friends and in Yourself

SOPHIA INSTITUTE PRESS®
Manchester, New Hampshire

The Art of Being a Good Friend: How to Bring Out the Best in Your Friends and in Yourself was originally published as *Friendship* in 1898 by the Fleming H. Revell Company, New York, Chicago, and Toronto. This 1999 edition by Sophia Institute Press contains minor editorial revisions to the original text.

Jacket design by Lorraine Bilodeau

The jacket atwork is a detail of Winslow Homer's *Breezing Up,* in the National Gallery of Art, Washington, DC (photo courtesy of SuperStock).

Sophia Institute Press®
Box 5284, Manchester, NH 03108
1-800-888-9344
www.sophiainstitute.com

Library of Congress Cataloging-in-Publication Data

Black, Hugh, b. 1868.
    [Friendship]
    The art of being a good friend : how to bring out the best in your friends and in yourself / Hugh Black.
        p.   cm.
    Originally published: Friendship. New York : F.H. Revell, 1898.
    Includes bibliographical references.
    ISBN 0-918477-62-X (pbk. : alk. paper)
    1. Friendship. 2. Friendship — Religious aspects — Christianity.
I. Title.
BJ1533.F8B53   1999
177'.62 — dc21   99-38478 CIP

99 00 01 02 03 04 05 9 8 7 6 5 4 3 2 1

To my friend
Hector Munro Ferguson
and to many other friends
who have made life rich

Contents

The Art of Being
a Good Friend

Chapter One

Appreciate the gift
of friendship

The idea, so common among the ancient writers, is not all a poetic conceit that the soul of a person is only a fragment of a larger whole and goes out in search of other souls in which it will find its true completion. We walk among worlds unrealized until we have learned the secret of love. We know this, and in our sincerest moments admit this, even though we are seeking to fill up our lives with other ambitions and other hopes.

It is more than a dream of youth that there may be here a satisfaction of the heart, without which, and in comparison with which, all worldly success is failure. In spite of the selfishness that seems to blight all life, our hearts tell us that there is possible a nobler relationship of disinterestedness and devotion. Friendship in its accepted sense is not the highest of the different grades in that relationship, but it has its place in the kingdom of love, and through it we bring ourselves into training for a still larger love. The natural person may be self-absorbed and self-centered, but, in a truer sense, it is natural for him to give up self and link his life to others. Hence the joy with which he makes the great discovery that he is something to another and another is everything to him. It is the higher-natural for which he has hitherto existed. It is a miracle, but it happens.

The Art of Being a Good Friend

The cynic may speak of the now obsolete sentiment of friendship, and he can find much to justify his cynicism. Indeed, on the first blush, if we look at the relative place the subject holds in ancient as compared with modern literature, we might say that friendship is a sentiment that is rapidly becoming obsolete. In the writings of the pagans, friendship takes a much larger place than it now receives. The subject bulks largely in the works of Plato, Aristotle, Epictetus, and Cicero. And among modern writers, it gets most importance in the writings of the more pagan-spirited, such as Montaigne.

In all the ancient systems of philosophy, friendship was treated as an integral part of the system. To the Stoic, it was a blessed occasion for the display of nobility and the native virtues of the human mind. To the Epicurean, it was the most refined of the pleasures which made life worth living.

In the *Nicomachean Ethics*, Aristotle makes it the culminating point and, out of ten books, gives two to the discussion of friendship. He makes it even the link of connection between his treatise on ethics and his companion treatise on politics. It is to him both the perfection of the individual life and the bond that holds states together. Not only is friendship a beautiful and noble thing for a person, but the realization of it is also the ideal for the state; for if citizens are friends, then justice, which is the great concern of all organized societies, is more than secured. Friendship is thus made the flower of ethics and the root of politics.

Plato also makes friendship the ideal of the state, where all have common interests and mutual confidence. And apart from its place of prominence in systems of thought, perhaps a finer list of beautiful sayings about friendship could be culled from ancient writers than from modern. Classical mythology also is full of instances of great friendship, which almost assumed the place of a religion itself.

It is not easy to explain why its part in Christian ethics is so small in comparison. The change is due to an enlarging of the thought and life of man. Modern ideals are wider and more impersonal, just as the modern conception of the state is wider. The Christian ideal of love even for enemies has swallowed up the narrower ideal of philosophical friendship. Then possibly also the instinct finds satisfaction elsewhere in the modern person. For example, marriage, in more cases now than ever before, supplies the need of friendship. Men and women are nearer in intellectual pursuits and in common tastes than they have ever been, and can be in a truer sense companions. And the deepest explanation of all is that the heart of man receives a religious satisfaction impossible before. Spiritual communion makes a person less dependent on human interchanges. When the heaven is as brass and makes no sign, men are thrown back on themselves to eke out their small stores of love.

☞

History and literature testify to selfless friendship

At the same time, friendship is not an obsolete sentiment. It is as true now as in Aristotle's time that no one would care to live without friends, even if he had all other good things. It is still necessary to our life in its largest sense. The danger of sneering at friendship is that it may be discarded or neglected, not in the interests of a more spiritual affection, but to minister to a debased, cynical self-indulgence. There is possible today, as ever, a generous friendship that forgets self. The history of the heart-life of man proves this. What records we have of such in the literature of every country! Peradventure for a good man, men have even dared to die.[1] Mankind has been glorified by countless silent heroisms, by unselfish service and sacrificing love.

Christ, who always took the highest ground in His estimate of people and never once put man's capacity for the noble on a low level, made the high-water mark of human friendship the standard of His own great action: "Greater love hath no man than this, that a man lay down his life for his friends."[2] This high-water mark has often been reached. People have given themselves to each other with nothing to gain, with no self-interest to serve, and with no keeping back part of the price. It is false to history to base life on selfishness, to leave out of the list of human motives the highest of all. The miracle of friendship has been too often enacted on this dull earth of ours to suffer us to doubt either its possibility or its wondrous beauty.

The classic instance of David and Jonathan represents the typical friendship.[3] They met and, at the meeting, knew each other to be nearer than kindred. By subtle elective affinity, they felt that they belonged to each other. Out of all the chaos of the time and the disorder of their lives, there arose for these two souls a new and beautiful world, where there reigned peace, love, and sweet content. It was the miracle of the death

---

[1] Cf. Rom. 5:7. The biblical quotations in these pages are based on the King James Version of the Old and New Testaments.

[2] John 15:13.

[3] Cf. 1 Sam. 18 ff.

of self. Jonathan forgot his pride, and David his ambition. It was as the smile of God which changed the world to them. One of them it saved from the temptations of a squalid court, and the other from the sourness of an exile's life. Jonathan's princely soul had no room for envy or jealousy. David's frank nature rose to meet the magnanimity of his friend.

In the kingdom of love, there was no disparity between the king's son and the shepherd boy. Such a gift as each gave and received is not to be bought or sold. It was the fruit of the innate nobility of both; it softened and tempered a very trying time for both. Jonathan withstood his father's anger to shield his friend; David was patient with Saul for his son's sake. They agreed to be true to each other in their difficult position. Close and tender must have been the bond, which had such fruit in princely generosity and mutual loyalty of soul. Fitting was the beautiful lament, when David's heart was bereaved at tragic Gilboa: "I am distressed for thee, my brother Jonathan; very pleasant hast thou been unto me: thy love to me was wonderful, passing the love of women."[4] Love is always wonderful, a new creation, fair and fresh to every loving soul. It is the miracle of spring to the cold, dull earth.

When Montaigne wrote his essay on friendship, he could do little but tell the story of his friend. The essay continually reverts to this, with joy that he had been privileged to have such a friend, with sorrow at his loss. It is a chapter of his heart. There was an element of necessity about it, as there is about all the great things of life. He could not account for it. It came to him without effort or choice. It was a miracle, but it happened.

[4] 2 Sam. 1:26.

"If a man should importune me to give a reason why I loved him, I can only answer, because it was he, because it was I." It was as some secret appointment of Heaven. They were both grown men when they first met, and death separated them soon. "If I should compare all my life with the four years I had the happiness to enjoy the sweet society of this excellent man, it is nothing but smoke; an obscure and tedious night from the day that I lost him. I have led a sorrowful and languishing life ever since. I was so accustomed to be always his second in all places and in all interests, that methinks I am now no more than half a man, and have but half a being." We would hardly expect such passion of love and regret from the easygoing, genial, garrulous essayist.

⁀

Friendship enlightens you

The joy that comes from a true communion of heart with another is perhaps one of the purest and greatest in the world, but its function is not exhausted by merely giving pleasure. Although we may not be conscious of it, there is a deeper purpose in it, an education in the highest arts of living. We may be enticed by the pleasure it affords, but its greatest good is got by the way. Even intellectually it means the opening of a door into the mystery of life.

Only love *understands* after all. It gives insight. We cannot truly know anything without sympathy, without getting out of self and entering into others. A person cannot be a true naturalist and observe the ways of birds and insects accurately unless he can watch long and lovingly. We can never know children unless we love them. Many of the chambers of the house of life are forever locked to us until love gives us the key.

Appreciate the gift of friendship

To learn to love all kinds of nobleness gives insight into the true significance of things, and gives a standard to settle their relative importance. An uninterested spectator sees nothing or, what is worse, sees wrongly. Most of our mean estimates of human nature in modern literature, our false realisms in art, and our stupid pessimisms in philosophy are due to an unintelligent reading of surface facts. People set out to note and collate impressions, and make perhaps a scientific study of slumdom, without genuine interest in the lives they see, and therefore without true insight into them. They miss the inwardness, which love alone can supply. If we look without love, we can see only the outside, the mere form and expression of the subject studied. Only with tender compassion and loving sympathy can we see the beauty even in the eye dull with weeping and in the fixed face pale with care. We will often see noble patience shining through them, and loyalty to duty, and virtues and graces unsuspected by others.

The divine meaning of a true friendship is that it is often the first unveiling of the secret of love. It is not an end in itself, but has most of its worth in what it leads to, the priceless gift of seeing with the heart rather than with the eyes. To love one soul for its beauty and grace and truth is to open the way to appreciate all beautiful and true and gracious souls, and to recognize spiritual beauty wherever it is seen.

We must have faith at least in the possibility of friendship. The cynical attitude is an offense. It is possible to find in the world true-hearted, loyal, and faithful dealing between one person and another. To doubt this is to doubt the divine in life. Faith in man is essential to faith in God. In spite of all deceptions and disillusionments, in spite of all the sham fellowships, in spite of the flagrant cases of self-interest and callous cruelty, we must keep clear and bright our faith in the possibilities of our nature. The person who hardens his heart because he has been imposed upon has no real belief in virtue and, with suitable circumstances, could become the deceiver instead of the deceived.

⌒

Friendship is a gift from God

The great miracle of friendship with its infinite wonder and beauty may be denied to us, and yet we may believe in it. To believe that it is possible is enough, even if, in its superbest form, it has never come to us. To possess it is to have one of the world's sweetest gifts.

Aristotle defines friendship as one soul abiding in two bodies. There is no explaining such a relationship, but there is no denying it. It has not deserted the world since Aristotle's time. Some of our modern poets have sung of it with as brave a faith as any poet of old. What splendid monuments to friendship we possess in Milton's "Lycidas" and Tennyson's *In Memoriam*! In both there is the recognition of the spiritual power of it, as well as the joy and comfort it brought. The grief is tempered by an awed wonder and a glad memory.

The finest feature of Rudyard Kipling's work — and it is a constant feature of it — is the comradeship between commonplace soldiers of no high moral or spiritual attainment, and yet it is the strongest force in their lives, and on occasion makes heroes of them. We feel that their faithfulness to each other is almost the only point at which their souls are reached. The threefold cord of his soldiers, vulgar in mind and common in thought as they are, is a cord that we feel is not easily broken, and it is their friendship and loyalty to each other that save them from utter vulgarity.

In the poetry of Walt Whitman, there is the same insight into the force of friendship in ordinary life, with added wonder at the miracle of it. He is the poet of comrades and sings the song of companionship more than any other theme. He ever comes back to the lifelong love of comrades. The mystery and the beauty of it impressed him:

> O tan-faced prairie-boy,
> Before you came to camp came many a welcome gift,
> Praises and presents came and nourishing food,
>   till at last among the recruits
> *You* came, taciturn, with nothing to give —
>   we but looked on each other,
> When lo! more than all the gifts of the world
>   you gave me.

After all, in spite of the vulgar materialism of our day, we do feel that the spiritual side of life is the most important and brings the only true joy. And friendship in its essence is spiritual. It is the free, spontaneous outflow of the heart and is a gift from the great Giver.

Friends are born, not made. At least it is so with the higher sort. The marriage of souls is a heavenly mystery, which we cannot explain and which we need not try to explain. The method by which it is brought about differs very much from friendship to friendship, and depends largely on temperament. Some friendships grow and ripen slowly and steadily with the years. We cannot tell where they began, or how. They have become part of our lives, and we just accept them with sweet content and glad confidence. We have discovered that somehow we are rested, and inspired, by a certain companionship, and that we understand and are understood easily.

Or it may come like love at first sight, by the thrill of elective affinity. This latter is the more uncertain and needs to be tested and corrected by the trial of the years that follow. It has to be found out whether it is really spiritual kinship or mere emotional impulse. It is a matter of temper and character. A naturally reserved person finds it hard to open his heart, even when his instinct prompts him, while a sociable, responsive nature is easily companionable. It is not always this quick attachment, however, that wears best, and that is the reason youthful friendships have the character of being so fickle. They are due to a natural instinctive delight in society. Most young people find it easy to be agreeable and are ready to place themselves under new influences.

Whatever the method by which a true friendship is formed, whether the growth of time or the birth of sudden sympathy, there seems, on looking back, to have been an element of necessity. It is a sort of predestined spiritual relationship. We speak of a person meeting his fate, and we speak truly. When we look back, we see it to be like destiny; life converged to life, and there was no getting out of it, even if we wished it. It is not that we made a choice, but that the choice made us. If it has come gradually, we waken to the presence of the force that has been in our lives, and has come into them never hasting but never resting, until now we know it to be an eternal possession. Or, as we are going about other business, never dreaming of the thing that occurs, the unexpected happens; on the road, a light shines on us, and life is never the same again.

In one aspect, faith is the recognition of the inevitableness of Providence, and when it is understood and accepted, it brings a great consoling power into the life. We feel that we are in the hands of a Love that orders our ways, and the knowledge means serenity and peace. The element of fate in friendship is gratefully accepted, as is the element of fate in birth. To the faith that sees love in all creation, all life becomes harmony, and all sorts of loving relationships among men seem to be part of the natural order of the world. Indeed, such miracles are only to be looked for and, if absent from the life of man, would make it hard to believe in the love of God.

☞

Friendship calls for humility and selflessness

The world thinks we idealize our friend and tells us that love is proverbially blind. Not so: it is only love that sees, and thus can "win the secret of a weed's plain heart." Only we who love see what dull eyes never see at all. If we wonder what another person sees in his friend, it should be the wonder of humility, not the supercilious wonder of pride. He sees something that we are not permitted to witness. Beneath and among what looks only like worthless slag, there may glitter the pure gold of a fair character. That anybody in the world should love us, and to see in us not what colder eyes see, not even what we are, but what we may be, should of itself make us humble and gentle in our criticism of others' friendships. Our friends see the best in us and, by that very fact, call forth the best from us.

The great difficulty in this whole subject is that the relationship of friendship should so often be one-sided. It seems strange that there should be so much unrequited affection in the world. It seems almost impossible to get a completely balanced union. One gives so much more and has to be content to get so much less. One of the most humiliating things in life is when another seems to offer his friendship lavishly and we are unable to respond. So much love seems to go a-begging. So few attachments seem complete. So much affection seems unrequited.

But are we sure it is unrequited? The difficulty is caused by our common selfish standards. Most people, if they had their choice, would prefer to be loved rather than to love, if only one of the alternatives were permitted. That springs from the root of selfishness in human nature, which makes us think that possession brings happiness. But the glory of life is to love, not to be loved; to give, not to get; to serve, not to be served. It may not be our fault that we cannot respond to the offer of friendship or love, but it is our misfortune. The secret is revealed to the other and hidden from us. The gain is to the other, and the loss is to us. The miracle is the love, and to the lover comes the wonder of it, and the joy.

Chapter Two

Cultivate your
friendships with care

The book of Proverbs might almost be called a treatise on friendship, so full is it of advice about the sort of person a young person should consort with and the sort of person he should avoid. It is full of shrewd, prudent, and wise, sometimes almost worldly wise, counsel.

It is caustic in its satire about false friends and about the way in which friendships are broken. "The rich hath many friends,"[5] it says with an easily understood implication concerning their quality. "Every man is a friend to him that giveth gifts,"[6] is its sarcastic comment on the ordinary motives of mean men. Its picture of the plausible, fickle, lip-praising, and time-serving person, who "blesseth his friend with a loud voice, rising early in the morning," is a delicate piece of satire.[7] The fragile connections among men, as easily broken as mended pottery, get illustration in the mischief-maker who loves to divide men: "A whisperer separateth chief friends."[8] There is keen irony here over the quality of ordinary friendship, as well as condemnation of the talebearer and his sordid soul.

[5] Prov. 14:20.
[6] Prov. 19:6.
[7] Prov. 27:14.
[8] Prov. 16:28.

This cynical attitude is so common that we hardly expect such a shrewd book to speak heartily of the possibilities of human friendship. Its object rather is to put youth on its guard against the dangers and pitfalls of social life. It gives sound advice about avoiding becoming surety for a friend. It warns against the tricks, cheats, and bad faith that swarmed in the streets of a city then, as they do still. It laughs, a little bitterly, at the thought that friendship can be as common as the eager, generous heart of youth imagines. It almost sneers at the gullibility of men in this whole matter. Yet there is no book, even in classical literature, that so exalts the idea of friendship and is so eager to have it truly valued and carefully kept.

The worldly wise warnings are, after all, in the interests of true friendship. To condemn hypocrisy is not, as is so often imagined, to condemn religion. To spurn the spurious is not to reject the true. A sneer at folly may be only a covert argument for wisdom. Satire is negative truth. The unfortunate thing is that many who begin with the prudential worldly wise philosophy end there. They never get past the sneer.

Not so this wise book. Despite its insight into man's weakness and its frank denunciation of the common masquerade of friendship, it speaks of true friendship in words of beauty never surpassed in the many appraisements of this subject. "A friend loveth at all times, and is a brother born for adversity. Faithful are the wounds of a friend. Ointment and perfume rejoice the heart; so doth the sweetness of a man's friend by hearty counsel. Thine own friend and thy father's friend forsake not."[9] These are not the words of a cynic who has lost faith in man.

[9] Prov. 17:17, 27:6, 9, 10.

True, this golden friendship is not a common thing to be picked up in the street. It would not be worth much if it were. Like wisdom, it must be sought for as for hidden treasure, and to keep it demands care and thought. To think that every goose is a swan, that every new comrade is the person of your own heart, is to have a very shallow heart. Every casual acquaintance is not a hero. There are pearls of the heart, which cannot be thrown to swine.[10]

Until we learn what a sacred thing a true friendship is, it is futile to speak of the culture of friendship. The person who wears his heart on his sleeve cannot wonder if daws peck at it. There ought to be a sanctuary, to which few receive admittance. It is great innocence, or great folly — and in this connection the terms are almost synonymous — to open our arms to everybody to whom we are introduced.

The book of Proverbs, as a manual on friendship, gives as shrewd and caustic warnings as are needed, but it does not go to the other extreme and say that all men are liars, that there are no truth and faithfulness to be found. To say so is to speak in haste. "There is a friend that sticketh closer than a brother, says this wisest of books."[11] There is possible such a blessed relationship, a state of love and trust and generous comradeship, where a person feels safe to be himself, because he knows that he will not easily be misunderstood.

The word *friendship* has been abased by being applied to low and unworthy uses, and so there is plenty of copy still to be gotten from life by the cynic and the satirist. The sacred name

[10] Cf. Matt. 7:6.
[11] Prov. 18:24.

of friend has been bandied about so that it runs the risk of losing its true meaning.

☞

Friendship requires effort

It is useless to speak of cultivating the great gift of friendship unless we make clear to ourselves what we mean by a friend. We make connections and acquaintances, and call them friends. We have few friendships, because we are not willing to pay the price of friendship.

If we think it is not worth the price, that is another matter and is quite an intelligible position, but we must not use the word in different senses and then rail at fate because there is no miracle of beauty and joy about our sort of friendship.

Like all other spiritual blessings, it comes to all of us at some time or other and, like them, is often let slip. We have the opportunities, but we do not make use of them. Most people make friends easily enough; few keep them. They do not give the subject the care, thought, and trouble it requires and deserves. We want the pleasure of society without the duty. We would like to get the good of our friends without burdening ourselves with any responsibility about keeping them friends.

The most common mistake we make is that we spread our friendship over a mass and have no depth of heart left. We lament that we have no staunch, faithful friend, when we have really not expended the love that produces such. We want to reap where we have not sown, the fatuousness of which we should see as soon as it is mentioned. "She that asks her dear five hundred friends"[12] (as William Cowper satirically describes

[12] William Cowper, *The Task*, Bk. 2, line 642.

a well-known type) cannot expect the exclusive affection that she has not given.

The secret of friendship is just the secret of all spiritual blessing. The way to get is to give. In the end, the selfish can never get anything but selfishness. The hard find hardness everywhere. As you mete, it is meted out to you.

Some have a genius for friendship. That is because they are open, responsive, and unselfish. They truly make the most of life, for, apart from their special joys, even intellect is sharpened by the development of the affections. No material success in life is comparable to success in friendship. We really do ourselves harm by our selfish standards.

There is an old Latin proverb,[13] expressing the worldly view that says that it is not possible for a person to love and at the same time to be wise. This is true only when wisdom is made equal to prudence and selfishness, and when love is made the same. Rather, it is never given to a person to be wise in the true and noble sense until he is carried out of himself in the purifying passion of love or the generosity of friendship. The self-centered being cannot keep friends even when he makes them; his selfish sensitiveness is always in the way, like a diseased nerve ready to be irritated.

The culture of friendship is a duty, as every gift represents a responsibility. It is also a necessity, for, without watchful care, it can no more remain with us than can any other gift. Without culture, it is at best only a potentiality. We may let it slip, or we can use it to bless our lives. The miracle of friendship, which came at first with its infinite wonder and beauty, wears

---

[13] *Non simul cuiquam conceditur, amare et sapere.*

off, and the glory fades into the light of common day. The early charm passes, and the soul forgets the first exaltation.

We are always in danger of mistaking the common for the commonplace. We must not look upon it merely as the great luxury of life, or it will cease to be even that. It begins with emotion, but if it is to remain, it must become a habit. Habit is fixed when an accustomed thing is organized into life; and, whatever may be the genesis of friendship, it must become a habit, or it is in danger of passing away as other impressions have done before.

Friendship needs delicate handling. We can ruin it by stupid blundering at the very birth, and we can kill it by neglect. It is not every flower that has vitality enough to grow in stony ground.

Lack of reticence, which is only the outward sign of lack of reverence, is responsible for the death of many a fair friendship. Worse still, it is often blighted at the very beginning by the insatiable desire for piquancy in talk, which can forget the sacredness of confidence. "An acquaintance grilled, scored, devilled, and served with mustard and cayenne pepper, excites the appetite; whereas a slice of cold friend with currant jelly is but a sickly, unrelishing meat."[14] Nothing is given to the person who is not worthy to possess it, and the shallow heart can never know the joy of a friendship, for the keeping of which he is not able to fulfill the essential conditions. Here also it is true that from the one who has not is taken away even that which he has.[15]

[14] William Makepeace Thackeray, *Roundabout Papers.*
[15] Cf. Matt. 13:12.

Friends must cultivate sympathy

The method for the culture of friendship finds its best and briefest summary in the Golden Rule. To do to and for your friend what you would have him do to and for you is a simple compendium of the whole duty of friendship. The very first principle of friendship is that it is a mutual thing, as among spiritual equals, and therefore it claims reciprocity, mutual confidence, and faithfulness. There must be sympathy to keep in touch with each other, but sympathy needs to be constantly exercised. It is a channel of communication that has to be kept open, or it will soon be clogged and closed.

The practice of sympathy may mean the cultivation of similar tastes, although that will almost naturally follow from the fellowship. But to cultivate similar tastes does not imply either absorption of one of the partners, or the identity of both. Rather, part of the charm of the friendship lies in the difference that exists in the midst of agreement. What is essential is that there should be a real desire and a genuine effort on the part of friends to understand each other. It is well worthwhile taking pains to preserve a relationship so full of blessing to both.

Here, as in all connections among people, there is also ample scope for patience. When we think of our own need for the constant exercise of this virtue, we will admit its necessity for others. After the first flush of communion has passed, we see in a friend things that detract from his worth and perhaps things that irritate us. This is only to say that no one is perfect. With tact, tenderness, and patience, it may be given us to help to remove what may be flaws in a fine character. In any case, it is foolish to forget the great virtues of our friend in fretful irritation at a few blemishes. We can keep the first ideal in our memory, even if we know that it is not yet an actual fact. We must not let our friendship be coarsened, but must keep it sweet and delicate, so that it may remain a refuge from the coarse world, a sanctuary where we leave criticism outside and can breathe freely.

⁂

Friendship requires trust

Trust is the first requisite for making a friend. How can we be anything but alone if our attitude toward men is one of armed neutrality, if we are suspicious, assertive, querulous, and overcautious in our advances? Suspicion kills friendship. There must be some magnanimity and openness of mind before a friendship can be formed. We must be willing to give ourselves freely and unreservedly.

Some find it easier than others to make advances, because they are naturally more trustful. A beginning has to be made somehow, and if we are moved to enter into personal association with another, we must not be too cautious in displaying our feeling. If we stand off in cold reserve, the ice, which trembled to thawing, is gripped again by the black hand of frost. There may be a golden moment that has been lost through a foolish reserve. We are so afraid of giving ourselves away cheaply — and it is a proper enough feeling, the value of which we learn through sad experience — but on the whole, perhaps the warm nature, which acts on impulse, is of a higher type than the overcautious nature, ever on the watch lest it commit itself. We can do nothing with each other, we cannot even do business with each other, without a certain amount of trust. Much more necessary is it in the beginning of a deeper relationship.

⁓

Faithfulness maintains friendship

And if trust is the first requisite for making a friend, *faithfulness* is the first requisite for keeping him. The way to have a friend is to be a friend. Faithfulness is the fruit of trust. We must be ready to lay hold of every opportunity that occurs of serving our friend. To most of us, life is made up of little things, and many a friendship withers through sheer neglect. Hearts are alienated, because each is waiting for some great occasion for displaying affection. The great spiritual value of friendship is the opportunity it affords for service, and if these are neglected, it is only to be expected that the gift should be taken from us.

Friendship, which begins with sentiment, will not live and thrive on sentiment. There must be loyalty, which finds expression in service. It is not the greatness of the help, or the intrinsic value of the gift, that gives it its worth, but the evidence it is of love and thoughtfulness.

Attention to detail is the secret of success in every sphere of life, and little kindnesses, little acts of considerateness, little appreciations, and little confidences are all that most of us are called on to perform, but they are all that are needed to keep a friendship sweet. Such thoughtfulness keeps our sentiment in evidence to both parties. If we never show our kind feeling, what guarantee has our friend, or even ourselves, that it exists? Faithfulness in deed is the outward result of constancy of soul. If there has come to us the miracle of friendship, if there is a soul to which our soul has been drawn, it is surely worthwhile being loyal and true.

Through the little occasions for helpfulness, we are training for the great trial, if it should ever come, when the fabric of friendship will be tested to the very foundation. The culture of friendship, and its abiding worth, never found nobler expression than in the beautiful proverb "A friend loveth at all times, and a brother is born for adversity."[16]

Most people do not deserve such a gift from Heaven. They look upon it as a convenience and accept the privilege of love without the responsibility of it. They even use their friends for their own selfish purposes and so never have true friends.

Some people shed friends at every step they rise in the social scale. It is mean and contemptible merely to use others so long as they further one's personal interests. But there is a nemesis on such heartlessness. To such can never come the ecstasy and comfort of mutual trust. This worldly policy can never truly succeed. It stands to reason that they cannot have brothers born for adversity and cannot count on the joy of the love that loves at all times, for they do not possess the quality that secures it. To act on the worldly policy, to treat a friend as if he might become an enemy, is of course to be friendless. To sacrifice a tried and trusted friend for any personal advantage of gain or position is to deprive our own heart of the capacity for friendship.

The passion for novelty will sometimes lead a person to act like this. Some shallow minds are ever afflicted by a craving for new experiences. They sit very loosely to the past. They are the easy victims of the untried and yearn perpetually for novel sensations. In this matter of friendship, they are ready to

[16] Prov. 17:17.

forsake the old for the new. They are always finding a swan in every goose they meet. They have their reward in a widowed heart. Says Shakespeare in his great manner:

> Those friends thou hast, and their adoption tried,
> Grapple them to thy soul with hoops of steel,
> But do not dull thy palm with entertainment
> Of each new-hatched, unfledged comrade.[17]

The culture of friendship must pass into the consecration of friendship if it is to reach its goal. It is a natural evolution. Friendship cannot be permanent unless it becomes spiritual. There must be fellowship in the deepest things of the soul, community in the highest thoughts, and sympathy with the best endeavors. We are bartering the priceless boon if we are looking on friendship merely as a luxury and not as a spiritual opportunity. It is, or can be, an occasion for growing in grace, for learning love, for training the heart to patience and faith, and for knowing the joy of humble service. We are throwing away our chance if we are not striving to be an inspiring and healthful environment to our friend. We are called to be our best to our friend, so that he may be his best to us, bringing out what is highest and deepest in the nature of both.

Human friendship leads to love for God

The culture of friendship is one of the approved instruments of culture of the heart, without which a person has not truly come into his kingdom. It is often only the beginning, but through tender and careful culture, it may be an education

[17] William Shakespeare, *Hamlet*, Act 1, scene 3.

for the larger life of love. It broadens out in ever-widening circles, from the particular to the general, and from the general to the universal — from the individual to the social, and from the social to God.

The test of religion is ultimately a very simple one. If we do not love those whom we have seen, we cannot love those whom we have not seen. All our sentiment about people at a distance, our heart-stirrings for the distressed and oppressed, and our prayers for the heathen are pointless and fraudulent if we are neglecting the occasions for service at hand. If we do not love our brethren here, how can we love our brethren elsewhere, except as a pious sentimentality? And if we do not love those we have seen, how can we love God, whom we have not seen?[18]

This is the highest function of friendship and the reason it needs thoughtful culture. We should be led to God by the joy of our lives as well as by the sorrow, by the light as well as by the darkness, by human friendship as well as by human loneliness. He is the Giver of every good gift. We wound His heart of love when we sin against love. The more we know of Christ's spirit and the more we think of the meaning of God's fathomless grace, the more will we be convinced that the way to please the Father and to follow the Son is to cultivate the graces of kindliness and gentleness and tenderness, to give ourselves to the culture of the heart. Not in the ecclesiastical arena, not in polemic for a creed, and not in self-assertion and disputing do we please our Master best, but in the simple service of love.

[18] Cf. 1 John 4:20.

Cultivate your friendships with care

To seek the good of men is to seek the glory of God. They are not two things, but one and the same. To be a strong hand in the dark to another in the time of need, to be a cup of strength to a human soul in a crisis of weakness, is to know the glory of life. To be a true friend, saving his faith in man, and making him believe in the existence of love, is to save his faith in God. And such service is possible for all. We need not wait for the great occasion and for the exceptional opportunity. We can never be without our chance, if we are ready to keep the miracle of love green in our hearts by humble service.

> The primal duties shine aloft like stars.
> The charities that soothe and heal and bless,
> Are scattered at the feet of man like flowers.

Chapter Three

Let your friendships bear fruit

In our utilitarian age, things are judged by their practical value. Men ask of everything, "What is its use?" Nothing is held to be outside criticism — neither the law because of its authority, nor religion because of its sacredness. Every relationship in life also has been questioned and is asked to show the reason of its existence. Even some relationships such as marriage, for long held to be above question, are put into the crucible.

On the whole, it is a good spirit, although it can be abused and carried to an absurd extreme. Criticism is inevitable and ought to be welcomed, provided we are careful about the true standard to apply. When we judge a thing by its use, we must not have a narrow view of what utility is. Usefulness to man is not confined to mere material values. The common standards of the marketplace cannot be applied to the whole of life. The things that cannot be bought cannot be sold, and the keenest appraisers would be puzzled to put a price on some of these unmarketable wares.

When we seek to show what are the fruits of friendship, we may be said to put ourselves in line with the critical spirit of our age. But even if it were proven that a person could make more of his life materially by himself, if he gave no hostages to fortune, it would not follow that it is good to disentangle oneself from the common human bonds, for our caveat would here apply, that utility is larger than mere material gain.

But even from this point of view, friendship justifies itself. "Two are better than one, because they have a good reward for their labor."[19] The principle of association in business is now accepted universally. It is found even to pay, to share work and profit. Most of the world's business is done by companies, partnerships, or associated endeavor of some kind. And the closer the intimacy between the persons so engaged, the intimacy of common desires and common purposes, mutual respect and confidence, and, if possible, friendship, the better chance there is for success. Two are better than one from the point of view even of the reward of each, and a threefold cord is not quickly broken, when a single strand would snap.

When men first learned, even in its most rudimentary sense, that union is strength, the dawn of civilization began. For offense and for defense, the principle of association early proved itself the fittest for survival. The future is always with Isaac, not with Ishmael, with Jacob, not with Esau. In everything this is seen, in the struggle of races, or trade, or ideas. Even as a religious method to make an impact on the world, it is true. John of the Desert[20] touched here a life, and there a life. Jesus of Nazareth, seeking disciples, founding a society, moved the world to its heart.

It is not necessary to labor this point, that two are better than one, to a commercial age like ours, which, whatever it

[19] Eccles. 4:9.

[20] Possibly St. John of Egypt (d. 394), desert hermit known for his miraculous healings and his prophecies. — ED.

does not know, at least knows its arithmetic. We would say that it is self-evident, that, by the law of addition, it is double and, by the law of multiplication, twice the number. But it is not so exact as that, nor so self-evident.

When we are dealing with people, our ready-reckoner rules do not work out correctly. In this region, one and one are not always two. They are sometimes more than two and sometimes less than two. Union of all kinds, which may be strength, may be weakness. It was not until Gideon had weeded out his army, once and twice, that he was promised victory.[21] The fruits of friendship may be corrupting and unspeakably evil to the life. The reward of the labor of two may be less than that of one. The boy pulling a barrow is lucky if he gets another boy to shove the barrow from behind, but if the boy behind not only ceases to shove, but sits on the barrow, the last end is worse than the first. A threefold cord with two of the strands rotten is worse than a single sound strand, for it deceives one into putting too much weight on it.

In social economics, it is evident that society is not merely the sum of the units that compose it. Two are better than one not merely because the force is doubled. It may even be said that two are better than two. Two together mean more than two added singly, for a new element is introduced that increases the power of each individually.

The truth of this is seen in the relationship of friends. Each gives to the other, and each receives, and the fruit of the interchange is more than either in himself possesses. Every individual relationship has contact with a universal. To reach out to

[21] Judg. 7:2-7.

the fuller life of love is a divine enchantment, because it leads to more than itself and is the open door into the mystery of life. We feel ourselves united to the race and no longer isolated units, but in the sweep of the great social forces that mold mankind. Every bond that binds one person to another is a new argument for the permanence of life itself and gives a new insight into its meaning. Love is the pledge and the promise of the future.

Besides this cosmic and perhaps somewhat shadowy benefit, there are many practical fruits of friendship to the individual. These may be classified and subdivided almost endlessly, and indeed, in every special friendship, the fruits of it will differ according to the character and closeness of the tie and according to the particular gifts of each of the partners. One person can give to his friend some quality of sympathy or some kind of help, or can supply some social need that is lacking in his character or circumstances.

Perhaps it is not possible to get a better division of the subject than the three noble fruits of friendship that Bacon enumerates: peace in the affections, support of the judgment, and aid in all actions and occasions.

⌒

Friendship satisfies the heart

First of all, there is the *satisfaction of the heart*. We cannot live a self-centered life without feeling that we are missing the true glory of life. We were made for social relationships, if only that the highest qualities of our nature might have an opportunity for development. The joy that a true friendship gives reveals the existence of the want of it, perhaps previously unfelt. It is a sin against ourselves to let our affections wither. This sense of incompleteness is an argument in favor of its possible satisfaction; our need is an argument for its fulfillment. Our hearts demand love, as truly as our bodies demand food.

We cannot live among others suspicious, careful of our own interests, and fighting for our own hand, without doing dishonor and hurt to our own nature. To be for ourselves puts the whole world against us. To harden our heart hardens the heart of the universe.

We need sympathy, and therefore we crave friendship. Even the most perfect of the sons of men felt this need of communion of the heart. Christ, in one aspect the most self-contained of men, showed this human longing all through His life. He ever desired for enlargement of heart in His disciples, in an inner circle within the circle, in the household of Bethany.[22] "Will ye also go away?" He asked in the crisis of His career.[23] "Could ye not watch with me one hour?" He sighed in His great agony.[24] He was perfectly human and therefore felt the lack of friendship.

The higher our relationships with each other are, the closer is the communion demanded. Highest of all in the things of the soul, we feel that the true Christian life cannot be lived in the desert, but must be a life among others, and this is because it is a life of joy as well as of service. We feel that, for the rounding of our life and the completion of our powers, we need interchange with our kind. Stunted affections dwarf the

[22] Bethany was the home of Mary, Martha, and Lazarus, who were friends of Jesus.

[23] John 6:67.

[24] Matt. 26:40.

whole man. We live by admiration, hope, and love, and these can be developed only in the social life.

The sweetest and most stable pleasures also are never selfish. They are derived from fellowship, from common tastes, and from mutual sympathy. Sympathy is not a quality needed merely in adversity. It is needed as much when the sun shines.

Indeed, sympathy is more easily obtained in adversity than in prosperity. It is comparatively easy to sympathize with a friend's *failure*, when we are not so true-hearted about his success. When a person is down on his luck, he can be sure of at least a certain amount of good fellowship to which he can appeal. It is difficult to keep a little touch of malice, or envy, out of congratulations. It is sometimes easier to weep with those who weep than to rejoice with those who rejoice. This difficulty is felt not with people above us, or with little connection with us, but with our equals. When a friend succeeds, there may be a certain regret that has not always an evil root, but is due to a fear that he is getting beyond our reach, passing out of our sphere, and perhaps will not need or desire our friendship so much as before. It is a dangerous feeling to give way to, but, up to a certain point, it is natural and legitimate.

A perfect friendship would not have room for such grudging sympathy, but would rejoice more for the other's success than for his own. The envious, jealous person never can be a friend. His mean spirit of detraction and insinuating ill will kills friendship at its birth.

For true satisfaction of the heart, there must be a fount of sympathy from which to draw in all the vicissitudes of life. Sorrow asks for sympathy — aches to let its griefs be known and shared by a kindred spirit. To find such is to dispel the loneliness from life. To have a heart that we can trust, and into which we can pour our griefs, our doubts, and our fears, is already to take the edge from the grief, and the sting from doubt, and the shade from fear.

Joy also demands that its joy should be shared. The man who has found his sheep that was lost calls together his neighbors and bids them rejoice with him because he has found the sheep that was lost.[25] Joy is more social than grief. Some forms of grief desire only to creep away into solitude like a wounded beast to its lair, to suffer alone and to die alone. But joy finds its counterpart in the sunshine and the flowers and the birds and the little children, and enters easily into all the movements of life. Sympathy will respond to a friend's gladness, as well as vibrate to his grief. A simple generous friendship will thus add to the joy and will divide the sorrow.

The religious life, despite all the unnatural experiments of monasticism and its kindred ascetic forms, is preeminently a life of friendship. It is individual in its root and social in its fruits. It is when two or three are gathered that religion becomes a fact for the world.[26] The joy of religion will not be hidden and buried in a person's heart. "Come, see a man who told me all that ever I did,"[27] is the natural outcome of the first wonder and the first faith. It spreads from soul to soul by the impact of soul on soul, from the original impact of the great soul of God.

Christ's ideal is the ideal of a kingdom, people banded together in a common cause, under common laws, serving the

[25] Cf. Luke 15:4-6.
[26] Cf. Matt. 18:19.
[27] Cf. John 4:29.

same purpose of love. It is meant to take effect upon man in all his social relationships, in the home, in the city, and in the state. Its greatest triumphs have been made through friendship, and it, in turn, has ennobled and sanctified the bond. The growth of the kingdom depends on the sanctified working of the natural ties among people. It was so at the very start: John the Baptist pointed out the Christ to John the future apostle and to Andrew; Andrew found his own brother Simon Peter; Philip found Nathaniel; and so society, through its network of relations, took into its heart the new message. The man who has been healed must go and tell those who are at home, must declare it to his friends, and seek that they also should share in his great discovery.[28]

The very existence of the Church as a body of believers is due to this necessity of our nature that demands opportunity for the interchange of Christian sentiment. The deeper the feeling, the greater is the joy of sharing it with another. There is a strange felicity, a wondrous enchantment, that comes from true intimacy of heart and close communion of soul, and the result is more than mere fleeting joy. When it is shared in the deepest thoughts and highest aspirations, when it is built on a common Faith and lives by a common hope, it brings perfect peace. No friendship has done its work until it reaches the supreme satisfaction of spiritual communion.

⤙

Friendship assists your judgment

In addition to this satisfaction of the heart, friendship also gives *satisfaction of the mind*. Most people have a certain natural

---

[28] Cf. Mark 5:20.

diffidence in coming to conclusions and forming opinions for themselves. We rarely feel confident until we have secured the agreement of others in whom we trust. There is always a personal equation in all our judgments, so that we feel that they require to be amended by comparison with those of others. Doctors ask for a consultation when a case becomes critical. We all realize the advantage of taking counsel. To ask for advice is a benefit, whether we follow the advice or not. Indeed, the best benefit often comes from the opportunity of testing our own opinion and finding it valid. Sometimes the very statement of the case is enough to prove it one thing or the other.

An advantage is reaped from a sympathetic listener, apart altogether from whether our friend is able to elucidate the matter by his special sagacity or experience. Friends in counsel gain much intellectually. They acquire something approaching a standard of judgment and are enabled to classify opinions and to make up their minds more accurately and securely. Through talking a subject over with another, one gets fresh sidelights into it, new avenues open up, and the whole question becomes larger and richer.

We must have been struck with the brilliancy of our own conversation and the profundity of our own thoughts when we shared them with one with whom we were in sympathy at the time. The brilliancy was not ours; it was the reflex action that was the result of the communion. That is why the effect of different people upon us is different: one making us creep into our shell and making us unable almost to utter a word; another, through some strange magnetism, enlarging the bounds of our whole being and drawing the best out of us. The true insight, after all, is love. It clarifies the intellect and opens the eyes to much that was obscure.

Besides the subjective influence, there may be the great gain of honest counsel. A faithful friend can be trusted not to speak merely soft words of flattery. It is often the spectator who sees most of the game, and, if the spectator is at the same time keenly interested in us, he can have a more unbiased opinion than we can possibly have.

He may have to say that which may wound our self-esteem; he may have to speak for correction rather than for commendation, but "faithful are the wounds of a friend."[29] The flatterer will take good care not to offend our susceptibilities by too many shocks of wholesome truth-telling, but a friend will seek our good, even if he must say the thing we hate to hear at the time.

This does not mean that a friend should always be what is called plainspoken. Many take advantage of what they call a true interest in our welfare in order to rub gall into our wounds. The person who boasts of his frankness and of his hatred of flattery is usually not frank, but only brutal. A true friend will never needlessly hurt, but also will never, through cowardice, let occasions for correction slip. To speak the truth in love takes off the edge of unpleasantness, which so often is found in truth-speaking. And however the wound may smart, in the end, we are thankful for the faithfulness that directed it. "Let the righteous smite me; it shall be a kindness. And let him reprove me; it shall be an excellent oil."[30]

[29] Prov. 27:6.
[30] Ps. 141:5.

In our relations with each other, there is usually more advantage to be reaped from friendly encouragement than from friendly correction. True criticism does not consist, as so many critics seem to think, in depreciation, but in appreciation — in putting oneself sympathetically in another's position and seeking to value the real worth of his work. There are more lives spoiled by undue harshness than by undue gentleness. More good work is lost from want of appreciation than from too much of it; and certainly it is not the function of friendship to do the critic's work. Unless carefully repressed, such a spirit becomes censorious or, worse still, spiteful, and has often been the means of losing a friend. It is possible to be kind without giving crooked counsel or oily flattery; and it is possible to be true without magnifying faults or indulging in cruel rebukes.

☞

Friendship helps you in life's difficulties

Besides the joy of friendship and its aid in matters of counsel, a third of its noble fruits is the direct *help* it can give us in the difficulties of life. It gives strength to the character. It sobers and steadies through the responsibility for each other which it means. When men face the world together and are ready to stand shoulder to shoulder, the sense of comradeship makes each strong. This help may not often be called into play, but just to know that it is there if needed is a great comfort — to know that, if one falls, the other will lift him up. The very word *friendship* suggests kindly help and aid in distress. In *King Lear*, Shakespeare applies the word to an inanimate thing with this meaning of helpfulness: "Gracious, my lord, hard by here is a hovel: some *friendship* will it lend you 'gainst the tempest."

The Art of Being a Good Friend

Sentiment does not amount to much if it is not an inspiring force to lead to gentle and generous deeds when there is need. The fight is not so hard when we know that we are not alone, but that there are some who think of us, pray for us, and would gladly help us if they had the opportunity.

Comradeship is one of the finest facts, and one of the strongest forces, in life. A mere strong person, however capable, and however singly successful, is of little account by himself. There is no glamour of romance in his career. The kingdom of Romance belongs to David, not to Samson — to David, with his eager, impetuous, affectionate nature, for whom three men went in the jeopardy of life to bring him a drink of water, and all for love of him.[31] It is not the self-centered, self-contained hero who lays hold of us; it is ever the comradeship of heroes. Alexandre Dumas's Three Musketeers (and the Gascon who made a greater fourth), with their oath, "All for one, and one for all," inherit that kingdom of Romance, with all that ever have been tied in bands of love.

Robertson of Brighton, in one of his letters, tells how a friend of his had, through cowardice or carelessness, missed an opportunity of putting him right on a point with which he was charged, and so left him defenseless against slander. With his native sweetness of soul, he contents himself with the exclamation, "How rare it is to have a friend who will defend you thoroughly and boldly!" Yet that is just one of the loyal things a friend can do sometimes, when it would be impossible for a person himself to do himself justice with others. Some things that need to be said or done under certain circumstances

[31] Cf. 2 Sam. 23:15-16.

cannot be undertaken without indelicacy by the person concerned, and the keen instinct of a friend should tell him that
he is needed.

A little thoughtfulness would often suggest things that
could be done for our friends that would make them feel that
the tie that binds us to them is a real one. One is rich indeed
who possesses thoughtful, tactful friends, with whom he feels
safe when he is present and in whose hands his honor is secure
when he is absent. If there is no loyalty, there can be no great
friendship. Most of our friendships lack the distinction of
greatness, because we are not ready for little acts of service.
Without these, our love dwindles down to a mere sentiment
and ceases to be the inspiring force for good to both our
friend's life and ours that it was at the beginning.

The aid we may receive from friendship may be of an even
more powerful, because more subtle, nature than material
help. It may be a safeguard against temptation. The recollec-
tion of a friend whom we admire is a great force to save us from
evil and to prompt us to good. The thought of his sorrow in
any moral breakdown of ours will often nerve us to stand firm.
What would my friend think of me, if I did this or consented to
this meanness? Could I look him in the face again and meet
the calm, pure gaze of his eye? Would it not be a blot on our
friendship and draw a veil over our interchanges? A friendship
that does not elevate and does not help to nobility of conduct
and to strength of character is not worth the name. It should
give a new zest to duty and a new inspiration to all that is good.

Influence is the greatest of all human gifts, and we all have
it in some measure. There are some to whom we are something, if not everything. There are some who are grappled to

us with hoops of steel. There are some over whom we have ascendancy, or at least to whom we have access, who have opened the gates of the City of Mansoul to us, some we can sway with a word, a touch, or a look. It must always be a solemn thing for a person to ask what he has done with this awesome power of influence. For what has our friend to be indebted to us — for good or for evil? Have we put on his armor and sent him out with courage and strength to the battle? Or have we dragged him down from the heights to which he once aspired?

We are face-to-face here with the tragic possibilities of human relationships. In all friendship, we open the gates of the city, and those who have entered must be either allies in the fight or treacherous foes.

All the fruits of friendship, be they blessed or baneful, spring from this root of influence, and influence in the long run is the impress of our real character on other lives. Influence cannot rise above the level of our lives. The result of our friendship on others will ultimately be conditioned by the sort of person we are. It adds a very sacred responsibility to life. Here, as in other regions, a good tree brings forth good fruit, but a corrupt tree brings forth evil fruit.[32]

[32] Cf. Matt. 7:17.

Chapter Four

*Use discernment
in choosing friends*

Our responsibility for our friendships is not confined to making sure that our influence over others is for good. We have also a duty to ourselves. As we possess the gift of influence over others, so we, in turn, are affected by every life that touches ours. Influence is like an atmosphere exhaled by each separate personality.

Some men seem neutral and colorless, with no atmosphere to speak of. Some have a bad atmosphere, like the rank poisonous odor of noxious weeds, breeding malaria. If our moral sense were only keen and true, we would instinctively know them, as some children do, and dread their company.

Others have a good atmosphere; we can breathe there in safety and have a joyful sense of security. With some of these, it is a local delicate environment, sweet, suggestive, like the aroma of wild violets; we have to look, and sometimes to stoop, to get into its range. With some, it is like a pine forest, or a eucalyptus grove of warmer climes, which perfumes a whole countryside.

It is good to know such, Christ's little ones and Christ's great ones. They put oxygen into the moral atmosphere, and we breathe more freely for it. They give us new insight, fresh courage, and purer faith, and, by the impulse of their example, inspire us to nobler life.

The Art of Being a Good Friend

You can adopt the good qualities of your friend

There is nothing so important as the choice of friendship, for it both reflects character and affects it. A person is known by the company he keeps. This is an infallible test, for his thoughts, desires, ambitions, and loves are revealed here. He gravitates naturally to his congenial sphere. And it affects character, for it is the atmosphere he breathes. It enters his blood and makes the circuit of his veins.

"All love assimilates to what it loves." A person is molded into the likeness of the lives that come nearest him. It is at the point of the emotions that he is most impressionable. The material surroundings, the outside lot of a person, affects him, but after all, that is mostly on the outside; for the higher functions of life may be served in almost any external circumstances. But the environment of other lives, the communion of other souls, are far more potent facts. The nearer people are to each other, and the less disguise there is in their relationship, the more invariably will the law of spiritual environment act.

It seems a tragedy that people who see each other as they are become like each other, and often it *is* a tragedy. But the law carries as much hope in it as it does despair. If evil works havoc through it, good also persists through it. If we are hindered by the weakness of our associates, we are often helped by their goodness and sweetness. Contact with a strong nature inspires us with strength. Someone once asked Kingsley what was the secret of his strong, joyous life, and he answered, "I had a friend." If every evil man is a center of contagion, every good person is a center of healing. He provides an environment in which others can see God.

Goodness creates an atmosphere for other souls to be good. It is a priestly garment that has virtue even for the finger that touches it.[33] The earth has its salt, and the world has its light,[34] in the sweet souls, winsome lives, and Christlike characters to be found in it.

The choice of friends is therefore one of the most serious affairs in life, just because a person becomes molded into the likeness of what he loves in his friend.

From the purely selfish standard, every fresh tie we form means giving a new hostage to fortune and adding a new risk to our happiness. Apart from any moral evil, every intimacy is a danger of another blow to the heart. But if we desire fullness of life, we cannot help ourselves. A person may make many a friendship to his own hurt, but the isolated life is a greater danger still. Every relationship means risk, but we must take the risk; for while nearly all our sorrows come from our connection with others, nearly all our joys have the same source. We cannot help ourselves; for it is part of the great discipline of life. Rather, we need knowledge, care, and forethought to enable us to make the best use of the necessities of our nature. And foremost of these for importance is our choice of friends.

⌒

You must choose your friends carefully

We may err on one side by being too cautious and too exclusive in our attachments. We may be supercilious and disdainful in our estimate of men. Contempt always blinds the eyes. Every person is vulnerable somewhere, if only like Achilles in

[33] Cf. Luke 8:43-46.
[34] Cf. Matt. 5:13, 14.

the heel. The true secret of insight is not contempt, but sympathy. Disdain usually means putting all the eggs into one basket, when a smash spells ruin.

The other extreme is the attitude that easily makes many friends without much consideration of quality. We know the type of person who is friendly with everybody and a friend of none. He is "Hail, fellow, well met"[35] with every passing stranger, a boon companion of every wayfarer. He takes up with every sort of casual comrade and seeks to be on good terms with everybody. He makes what is called, with a little contempt, "good company" and is a favorite on all light occasions. His affections spread themselves out over a large expanse. He is easily consoled for a loss and easily attracted by a new attachment. And as he deals, so is he dealt with. Many like him; few quite trust him.

He makes many friends and is not particular about their quality. The law of spiritual environment plays upon him with its relentless force. He gives himself away too cheaply and opens himself to all sorts of influence. He is constantly laying himself in the way of temptation. His mind takes on the opinions of his set; his character assimilates itself to the forces that act on it. The evil example of some of his intimates gradually breaks down the barriers of past training and teaching. The desire to please a crowd means that principle is let slip, and conscience ceases to be the standard of action. His very friends are not true friends, being mostly of the fair-weather quality.

Although it may seem difficult to avoid either of these two extremes, it will not do to refuse to choose at all and leave

[35] Jonathan Swift, "My Lady's Lamentation."

things to chance. We drift into many of our connections with others, but the art of seamanship is tested by sailing, not by drifting. The subject of the choice of friendship is not advanced much by just letting them choose us. That is to become the victim, not the master, of our circumstances. And while it is true that we are acted on as much as we act, and are chosen as much as we choose, it is not permitted to anyone merely to be passive, except at great cost.

At the same time, in the mystery of friendship, we cannot say that we went about with a touchstone testing all we met until we found the one who would respond to our particular magnet. It is not that we said to ourselves, "Go to, we will choose a friend, and straightway made a distinct election to the vacant throne of our heart." From one point of view, we were absolutely passive. Things arranged themselves without effort, and, by some subtle affinity, we learned that we had gained a friend.

The history of every true friendship is the brief description of Emerson, "My friends have come to me unsought; the great God gave them to me." There was an element of necessity in this, as in all crises of life.

Does it therefore seem absurd and useless to speak about the choice of friendship at all? By no means, because the principles we set before ourselves will determine the kind of friends we have, as truly as if the whole initiative lay with us. We are chosen for the same reason for which we would choose. To try to separate the two processes is to make the same futile distinction, on a lower scale, so often made between choosing God and being chosen by Him. It is futile because the distinction cannot be maintained.

Besides, the value of having some definite principle by which to test friendship is not confined to the positive attachments made. The necessity for a system of selection is largely due to the necessity for rejection. The good and great intimacies of our life will perhaps come to us as the wind blows, we cannot tell how. But by regulating our course wisely, we will escape from hampering our life by mistakes, and weakening it with false connections. We ought to be courteous, kind, and gentle with all, but not to all can we open the sanctuary of our heart.

⌒

There are different degrees of friendship

We have a graduated scale of intimacy, from introduction and nodding acquaintance and speaking acquaintance, through an endless series of kinds of relationships to the perfect friendship. In counting up our gains and our resources, we cannot give them all the same value without deceiving ourselves. To expect loyalty and devotion from all alike is to court disappointment. Most misanthropic and cynical estimates of man are due to this mingled ignorance and conceit. We cannot look for undying affection from the crowd we may happen to have entertained to dinner or have rubbed shoulders with at business resorts or at social gatherings.

Many in life, as many are depicted in literature, have played the misanthrope, because they have discovered through adversity how many of their associates were fair-weather friends. In their prosperity, they encouraged toadying and sycophancy. They liked to have hangers-on who would flatter, and, when the east wind blows, they are indignant that their circle would prefer to avoid it.

Shakespeare's Timon of Athens is a typical misanthrope in his virtuous indignation at man's catlike love for comfort. In his prosperity, crowds of glass-faced flatterers bent before him and were made rich at Timon's nod. He wasted his substance in presents and hospitality, and bred a fine race of parasites and trencher-friends. When he spent all and began to be in want, no man gave unto him. The winter shower drove away the summer flies. He had loved the reputation for splendid liberality and lavish generosity, and had sought to be a little god among men, bestowing favors and receiving homage, all of which was only a more subtle form of selfishness.

When the brief day of prosperity had passed, men shut their doors against the setting sun. The smooth and smiling crowd dropped off with a shrug, and Timon went to the other extreme of misanthropy, declaimed against friendship, and cursed men for their ingratitude. But, after all, he got what he had paid for. He thought he had been buying the hearts of men and found that he had bought only their mouths, tongues, and eyes.

"He that loves to be flattered is worthy o' the flatterer."[36] For moral value, there is not much to choose between them. Rats are said to desert the sinking ship, which is not to be wondered at in rats. The choice of friendship does not mean the indiscriminate acceptance of all who are willing to assume the name of friend. A touch of east wind is good, not only to weed out the false and test the true, but also to brace a person to the stern realities of life. When we find that some of our intimates are dispersed by adversity, instead of raving against the world's

[36] William Shakespeare, *Timon of Athens*, Act 1, scene 1.

ingratitude like Timon, we should be glad that now we know exactly whom we can trust.

⁀

Friendship precludes using others

Another common way of choosing friends, and one that also meets with its own fitting reward, is the selfish method of valuing men according to their usefulness to us. To add to their credit or reputation, some are willing to include anybody in their list of intimates. For business purposes even, people will sometimes run risks by endangering the peace of their home and the highest interests of those they love; they are ready to introduce into their family circle people whom they distrust morally, because they think they can make some gain out of the connection.

All the stupid snobbishness and mean tuft-hunting so common are due to the same desire to make use of people in some way or other. It is an abuse of the word *friendship* to apply it to such social scrambling. Of course, even tuft-hunting may be only a perverted desire after what we think the best, a longing to get near those we consider of nobler nature and larger mind than common associates. It may be an instinctive agreement with Plato's definition of the wise man, as ever wanting to be with him who is better than himself. But in its usual form, it becomes an unspeakable degradation, inducing servility, lickspittle humility, and all the vices of the servile mind. There can never be true friendship without self-respect and unless soul meets soul free from self-seeking.

If we had higher standards for ourselves, if we lived to God and not to men, we would also find that in the truest sense we would live with men. We need not go out of our way to ingratiate ourselves with anybody. Nothing can make up for the loss of independence and native dignity of soul. It is not for a person, made in the image of God, to grovel and demean himself before his fellow creatures.

After all, it defeats itself, for there can be friendship only *between equals*. This does not mean equals in what is called social position, nor even in intellectual attainments — although these naturally have weight — but it means equality that has a spiritual source: "Can two walk together, except they be agreed?"[37]

Nor does it mean identity, nor even likeness. Indeed, for the highest unity, there must be difference, the difference of free beings, with will, conscience, and mind unhampered. We often make much of our differences, forgetting that really we differ, and *can* differ, only because we agree. Without many points of contact, there could be no divergence from these. Argument and contradiction of opinion are the outcome of difference, and yet for argument there is needed a common basis. We cannot even discuss unless we meet on some mental ground common to both disputants. So there may be — nay, for the highest union, there *must* be a great general conformity behind the distinctions, a deep underlying common basis beneath the unlikeness.

And for true union of hearts, this equality must have a spiritual source. If, then, there must be some spiritual affinity, agreement in what is best and highest in each, we can see the futility of most of the selfish attempts to make capital out of our friendship. Our friends will be, because they must be, our

[37] Amos 3:3.

equals. We can never have a nobler intimacy until we are made fit for it.

All connections based on selfishness, either on personal pleasure or on usefulness, are accidental. They are easily dissolved, because, when the pleasure or the utility ceases, the bond ceases; when the motive of the friendship is removed, the friendship itself disappears. The perfect friendship is grounded on what is permanent, on goodness, on character. It is of much slower growth, since it takes some time really to find out the truly lovable things in a life, but it is lasting, since the foundation is stable.

⁂

Avoid friendship with those of bad influence

The most important point, therefore, about the choice of friendship is that we should know what to reject. Countless attractions come to us on the lower plane. A person may be attracted by what his own conscience tells him is unworthy. He may have slipped gradually into companionship with some whose influence is even evil. He may have gotten, almost without his own will, into a set that is deteriorating his life and character. He knows the fruits of his weakness, in the lowering of the moral tone, in the slackening grip of the conscience, and in the looser flow of the blood. He has become pliant in will, feeble in purpose, and flaccid in character. Everyone has a duty to himself to be his own best self, and he can never be that under the spell of evil companionship.

Some men mix in doubtful company and say that they have no pharisaical exclusiveness, and even sometimes defend themselves by the example of Christ, who received sinners and ate with them. The comparison borders on blasphemy. It depends on the purpose for which sinners are received. Christ never joined in their sin, but went to save them from their sin; and wickedness could not lift its head in His presence.

Some seek to be initiated into the mysteries of iniquity, in idle or morbid curiosity, perhaps to write a realistic book, or to see "life," as it is called. There is often a prurient desire to explore the tracts of sin, as if information on such subjects meant wisdom. If men are honest with themselves, they will admit that they join the company of sinners for the relish they have for the sin. We must first obey the moral command to come out from among them and be separate,[38] before it is possible for us to meet them like Christ. Separateness of soul is the law of holiness. Of Christ, of whom it was said, "This man receiveth sinners," it was also said that He was "separate from sinners."[39] The knowledge of wickedness is not wisdom, neither is the counsel of sinners prudence. Most young people know the temptation here referred to, the curiosity to learn the hidden things and to have the air of those who know the world.

If we have gone wrong here, and have admitted into the sanctuary of our lives influences that make for evil, we must break away from them at all costs. The sweeter and truer relationships of our life should arm us for the struggle, the prayers of a mother, the sorrow of true friends. This is the fear, countless times, in the hearts of the folks at home when their boy leaves them to win his way in the city, the deadly fear that he should fall into evil habits and into the clutches of evil people. They know that there are people whose touch, whose words,

[38] 2 Cor. 6:17.
[39] Luke 15:2; Heb. 7:26.

whose very look, is contamination. To give them entrance into our lives is to submit ourselves to the contagion of sin.

༄

Friendship should have a spiritual basis

Friends should be chosen by a higher principle of selection than any worldly one of pleasure or usefulness, or by weak submission to the evil influences of our lot. They should be chosen for character, for goodness, for truth and trustworthiness, because they have sympathy with us in our best thoughts and holiest aspirations, because they have community of mind in the things of the soul. All other connections are fleeting and imperfect from the nature of the case. A relationship based on the physical withers when the first bloom fades; a relationship founded on the intellectual is only a little more secure, as it, too, is subject to caprice. All purely earthly partnerships, like all earthly treasures, are exposed to decay, the bite of the moth, and the stain of the rust,[40] and they must all have an end.

A young person may get opposing advice from two equally trusted counselors. One will advise him to cultivate the friendship of the clever, because they will afterward occupy places of power in the world. The other will advise him to cultivate the friendship of the good, because if they do not inherit the earth, they aspire to the heavens. If he knows the character of the two counselors, he will understand why they should look upon life from such different standpoints; and later on, he will find that while some of his friends were both clever and good, not one of the purely intellectual friendships remain to him. It does not afford a sufficient basis of agreement, to stand the

---

[40] Cf. Matt. 6:19.

wear and tear of life. The basis of friendship must be community of soul.

The only permanent severance of heart comes through lack of a common spiritual footing. If one soul goes up to the mountaintop and the other stays down among the shadows, if the two have not the same high thoughts, pure desires, and ideals of service, they cannot remain together except in form. Friends need not be identical in temperament and capacity, but they must be alike in sympathy. An unequal yoke becomes either an intolerable burden, or will drag one of the partners away from the path his soul at its best would have loved to tread.

> If you loved only what were worth your love,
> Love were clear gain, and wholly well for you.

If we choose our friends in Christ, we need not fear parting, neither here, nor ever, and we will have the secure joy and peace that come from having a friend who is as one's own soul.

Chapter Five

Recognize that friendship transcends death

As it is one of the greatest joys of life when a kindred soul is for the first time recognized and claimed, so it is one of the bitterest moments of life when the first rupture is made of the ties that bind us to other lives. Before it comes, it is hard to believe that it is possible, if we ever think of it at all. When it does come, it is harder still to understand the meaning of the blow. The miracle of friendship seemed too fair to carry in its bosom the menace of its loss. We knew, of course, that such things had been, and must be, but we never quite realized what it would be to be the victims of the common doom of man.

If it came only as a sudden pain that passes after its brief spasm of agony, it would not be so sore an affliction; but when it comes, it comes to stay. There remains a place in our hearts that is tender to every touch, and it is touched so often. We survive the shock of the moment easier than the constant reminder of our loss. The old familiar face, debarred to the sense of sight, can be recalled by a stray word, a casual sight, or a chance memory. The closer the relationship had been with a friend, the more things there are in our lives associated with him — things that we did together, places that we visited together, even thoughts that we thought together.

There seems no region of life where we can escape from the suggestions of memory. The sight of any little object can bring him back, with his way of speaking, with his tricks of gesture, with all the qualities for which we loved him, and for which we mourn him now. If the intimacy was due to mere physical proximity, the loss will be only a vague sense of uneasiness through the breakdown of long-continued habit; but if the two lives were woven into the same web, there must be ragged edges left, and it is a weary task to take up the threads again and find a new woof for the warp. The closer the connection has been, the keener is the loss. It comes back to us at the sight of the many things associated with him, and, even if we fill up our lives with countless distractions, the shadow creeps back to darken the world.

Sometimes there is the added pain of remorse that we did not appreciate enough the treasure we possessed. In thoughtlessness we accepted the gift; we had so little idea of the true value of his friendship; we loved so little and were so impatient. If only we had him back again; if only we had one more opportunity to show him how dear he was; if only we had another chance of proving ourselves worthy. We can hardly forgive ourselves that we were so cold and selfish. Self-reproach, the regret of the unaccepted opportunity, is one of the most common feelings after bereavement, and it is one of the most blessed.

Still, it may become a morbid feeling. It is a false sentimentalism that lives in the past and lavishes its tenderness on memory. It is difficult to say what is the dividing line between healthy sorrow and morbid sentiment. It seems a natural instinct that makes the bereaved care lovingly for the very grave, and that makes the mother keep locked up the little shoes worn by the little feet, relics hidden from the vulgar eye.

The instinct has become a little more morbid when it has preserved the room of a dead mother, with its decorations and ornaments as she left them. Beautiful as the instinct may be, there is nothing so dangerous as when our most natural feeling turns morbid.

It is always a temptation, which grows stronger the longer we live, to look back instead of forward, to bemoan the past, and thus deride the present and distrust the future. We must not forget our present blessings, the love we still possess, the gracious influences that remain, and, most of all, the duties that claim our strength. The loving women who went early in the morning to the sepulcher of the buried Christ were met with a rebuke: "Why seek ye the living among the dead?"[41] They were sent back to life to find Him, and sent back to life to do honor to His death. Not by ointments and spices, however precious, nor at the rock-hewn tomb, could they best remember their Lord, but out in the world, which, that morning, had seemed so cold and cheerless, and in their lives, which then had seemed not worth living.

Christianity does not condemn any natural human feeling, but it will not let these interfere with present duty and destroy future usefulness. It does not send men to search for the purpose of living in the graves of their dead hopes and pleasures. Its disciples must not attempt to live on the relics of even great incidents, among crucifixes and tombs. In the desert, the heart must reach forward to the Promised Land, and not back to Egypt. The Christian faith is for the future, because it believes in the God of the future. The world is not a lumber room, full

---

[41] Luke 24:5.

of relics and remembrances, over which to brood. We are asked to remember the beautiful past that was ours and the beautiful lives we have lost, by making the present beautiful like it and our lives beautiful like theirs. It is human to think that life has no future, if now it seems "full of griefs and graves." It comes like a shock to find that we must bury our sorrow, and come into contact with the hard world again, and live our common life once more.

The Christian learns to do it, not because he has a short memory, but because he has a long faith. The voice of inspiration is heard more often through the realities of life than through vain regrets and recluse dreams. The Christian life must be in its degree something like the Master's own life, luminous with His hope and surrounded by a bracing atmosphere that uplifts all who touch even its outer fringe.

Death should awaken you to life's solemn purpose

The great fact of life, nevertheless, is death, and it must have a purpose to serve and a lesson to teach. It seems to lose something of its impressiveness, because it is universal. The very inevitableness of it seems to kill thought, rather than induce it. It is only when the blow strikes home that we are pulled up and forced to face the fact. Theoretically there is a wonderful unanimity among people regarding the shortness of life and the uncertainty of all human relationships. The last word of the wise on life has ever been its fleetingness, its appalling changes, and its unexpected surprises. The only certainty of life is its uncertainty — its unstable tenure, its inevitable end. But practically we go on as if we could lay our plans, and mortgage time, without doubt or danger, until our feet are knocked from under us by some sudden shock, and we realize how unstable the equilibrium of life really is. The lesson of life is death.

The experience would not be so tragically universal if it had not a good and necessary meaning. For one thing, it should sober us and make our lives full of serious, solemn purpose. It should teach us to number our days, that we may apply our hearts to wisdom.[42] The person who has no place for death in his philosophy has not learned to live. The lesson of death is life.

On the whole, however, it is not our own liability to death that oppresses us. The fear of it to a brave person, not to speak of a person of faith, can be overcome. It is the fear of it for others whom we love that is its sting. And none of us can live very long without knowing in our own heart's experience the reality, as well as the terror, of death. This, too, has its meaning for us, to look at life more tenderly and touch it more gently. The pathos of life is only a forced sentiment to us if we have not felt the pity of life. To a sensitive soul, smarting with his own loss, the world sometimes seems full of graves and, for a time at least, makes him walk softly among others.

This is one reason why the making of new friends is so much easier in youth than later on. Friendship comes to youth seemingly without any conditions and without any fears. There is no past to look back at with much regret and some sorrow. We never look behind us *until we miss something.* Youth is satisfied with the joy of present possession. To the young, friendship comes as the glory of spring, a very miracle of beauty, a

[42] Cf. Ps. 90:12.

mystery of birth; to the old, it has the bloom of autumn, beautiful still, but with the beauty of decay. To the young, it is chiefly hope; to the old, it is mostly memory. The person who is conscious that he has lost the best of his days, the best of his powers, and the best of his friends naturally lives a good deal in the past.

Such a person is prepared for further losses; he has adjusted himself to the fact of death. At first, we cannot believe that it can happen to us and to our love; or, if the thought comes to us, it is an event too far in the future to ruffle the calm surface of our heart. And yet, it must come; from it none can escape. Most can remember a night of waiting, too stricken for prayer, too numb of heart even for feeling, vaguely expecting the blow to strike us out of the dark. A strange sense of the unreality of things came over us when the black wave submerged us and passed on. We went out into the sunshine, and it seemed to mock us. We entered again among the busy ways of people, and the roar of life beat upon our brain and heart:

> Yet in these ears, till hearing dies,
> One set slow bell will seem to toll,
> The passing of the sweetest soul
> That ever looked with human eyes.

Was it worthwhile to have linked our lives to other lives and laid ourselves open to such desolation? Would it not be better to go through the world without joining ourselves too closely to the fleeting bonds of other loves? Why deliberately add to our disabilities?

But it is not a disability; rather, the great purpose of all our living is to learn love, even though we must experience the pains of love as well as the joys. To cut ourselves off from this lot of the human would be to impoverish our lives and deprive ourselves of the culture of the heart, which, if a person has not learned, he has learned nothing. Whatever the risks to our happiness, we cannot stand out from the lot of the human without ceasing to be human in the only true sense.

It is not easy to solve the problem of sorrow. Indeed there is no solution to it, unless the individual soul works out its own solution. Most attempts at a philosophy of sorrow just end in high-sounding words. Explanations that profess to cover all the ground are as futile as the ordinary blundering attempts at comfort, which only charm ache with sound and patch grief with proverbs. The sorrow of our hearts is not appreciably lessened by argument. Any kind of philosophy — any wordy explanation of the problem — is at best poor comfort. It is not the problem that brings the pain in the first instance; it is the pain that brings the problem. The heart's bitterness is not allayed by an exposition of the doctrine of Providence. Rachel who weeps for her children, and the father whose little daughter lies dead at home,[43] are not to be appeased in their anguish by a nicely balanced system of thought. Nor is surcease of sorrow thus brought to the man to whom has come a bereavement, or a succession of bereavements, which makes him feel that all the glory and joy of life, its friendship and love and hope, have gone down into the grave, so that he can say:

> Three dead men have I loved
> And thou wert last of the three.

---

[43] Cf. Jer. 31:15; Matt. 2:18, 9:18.

At the same time, if it is true that there is a meaning in friendship, a spiritual discipline to educate the heart and train the life, it must also be true that there is equally a meaning in the eclipse of friendship. If we have enough faith to see death, in many senses, to be good, we will find out for ourselves why it is good. It may teach us just what we were in danger of forgetting, some omission in our lives that was making them shallow and poor. It may be a sight into the mystery of sin or a sight into the mystery of love. To one it comes with the lesson of patience, which is only a side of the lesson of faith; to another it brings the message of sympathy. As we turn the subject toward the light, there come gleams of color from different facets of it.

⌒

Death leads to fuller life

All life is an argument for death. We cannot persist long in the effort to live the Christian life without feeling the need for death. The higher the aims, and the truer the aspirations, the greater is the burden of living, until it would become intolerable. Sooner or later, we are forced to make the confession of Job: "I would not live always."[44] To live forever in this sordidness, to have no reprieve from the doom of sin, no truce from the struggle of sin, would be a fearful fate.

To the Christian, therefore, death cannot be looked on as evil — first, because it is universal, and it is universal because it is God-ordained. In St. Peter's in Rome, there are many tombs in which death is symbolized in its traditional form as a skeleton, with the fateful hourglass and the fearful scythe; death is the rude reaper, who cruelly cuts off life and all the joy

[44] Job 7:16.

of life. But there is one tomb in which death is sculptured as a sweet, gentle, motherly woman who takes her wearied child home to safer and surer keeping. It is a truer thought than the other. Death is a minister of God, doing His pleasure, and doing us good.

Again, death cannot be evil because it means a fuller life and therefore an opportunity for fuller and further service. Faith will not let a person hasten the climax; for it is in the hands of love, as he himself is. But death is the climax of life. For if all life is an argument for death, then so also all death is an argument for life.

Jowett says, in one of his letters, "I cannot sympathize in all the grounds of consolation that are sometimes offered on these melancholy occasions, but there are two things which have always seemed to me unchangeable: first, that the dead are in the hands of God, who can do for them more than we can ask or have; and secondly, with respect to ourselves, that such losses deepen our views of life, and make us feel that we would not always be here." These are two noble grounds of consolation, and they are enough.

⌒

You can maintain communion
with friends who have died

Death is the great argument for immortality. We cannot believe that the living, loving soul has ceased to be. We cannot believe that all those treasures of mind and heart are squandered in empty air. We will not believe it. When once we understand the meaning of the spiritual, we see the absolute certainty of eternal life; we need no arguments for the persistence of being.

To appear for a little time and then vanish away is the outward biography of all men, a circle of smoke that breaks, a bubble on the stream that bursts, a spark put out by a breath.

But there is another biography, a deeper and permanent one: the biography of the soul. Everything that *appears* vanishes away; that is its fate, the fate of the everlasting hills as well as of the vapor that caps them. But that which does not appear, the spiritual and unseen, which we in our folly sometimes doubt because it does not appear, is the only reality; it is eternal and does not pass away. The material in nature is only the garb of the spiritual, as speech is the clothing of thought. With our vulgar standards, we often think of the thought as the unsubstantial and the shadowy, and the speech as the real. But speech dies upon the passing wind; the thought alone remains. We consider the sound to be the music, whereas it is only the expression of the music, and it vanishes away.

Behind the material world, which waxes old as a garment, there is an eternal principle, the thought of God it represents. Above the sounds, there is the music that can never die. Beneath our lives, which vanish away, there is a vital thing: spirit. We cannot locate it and put our finger on it; that is why it is permanent. The things we can put our finger on are the things that appear and therefore the things that fade and die.

So, death to the spiritual mind is only *eclipse*. When there is an eclipse of the sun, it does not mean that the sun is blotted out of the heavens; it means only that there is a temporary obstruction between it and us. If we wait a little, it passes.

Love cannot die. Its forms may change, even its objects, but its life is the life of the universe. It is not death, but sleep; not loss, but eclipse. The love is only transfigured into something more ethereal and heavenly than ever before. Happy to have friends on earth, but happier to have friends in Heaven.

And it need not be even eclipse, except in outward form. Communion with the unseen can mean true correspondence with all we have loved and lost, if only our souls are responsive. The highest love is not starved by the absence of its object; it rather becomes more tender and spiritual, with more of the ideal in it. Ordinary affection, on a lower plane, dependent on physical attraction, or on the earthly side of life, naturally crumbles to dust when its foundation is removed. But love is independent of time and space and, as a matter of fact, is purified and intensified by absence.

Separation of friends is not a physical thing. Lives can be sundered as if divided by infinite distance, even though materially they are near each other. This tragedy is often enough enacted in our midst.

The converse is also true, so friendship does not really lose by death: it lays up treasure in Heaven[45] and leaves the very earth a sacred place, made holy by happy memories. "The ruins of Time build mansions in Eternity," said William Blake, speaking of the death of a loved brother with whose spirit he never ceased to converse.

The spiritual world is not outside this earth. It includes it and pervades it, finding a new center for a new circumference in every loving soul that has eyes to see the Kingdom. So, to hold commerce with the dead is not a mere figure of speech. Heaven lies about us not only in our infancy, but all our lives. We blind ourselves with dust and, in our blindness, lay hold

[45] Cf. Matt. 6:20.

feverishly of the outside of life, mistaking the fugitive and eva-
nescent for the truly permanent. If we only used our capaci-
ties, we would take a more enlightened view of death. We
would see it to be the entrance into a more radiant and more
abundant life, not only for the friend who goes first, but for the
one left behind.

Spiritual communion cannot possibly be interrupted by a
physical change. It is because there is so little of the spiritual
in our ordinary interchanges that death means silence and an
end to communion. There is a picture of death that, when
looked at with the ordinary perspective, seems to be a hideous
skull, but when seen near at hand, is composed of flowers, with
the eyes, in the seemingly empty sockets of the skull, formed
by two fair faces of children. Death at a distance looks horri-
ble, the ghastly specter of the race; but with the near vision, it
is beautiful with youth and flowers, and, when we look into its
eyes, we look into the stirrings of life.

Love is the only permanent relationship among men, and
the permanence is not an accident of it, but is of its very essence. When released from the mere magnetism of sense, instead of ceasing to exist, it only then truly comes into its
largest life. If our life were more a life in the spirit, we would be
sure that death can be at the worst only the eclipse of friendship. Tennyson felt this truth in his own experience and expressed it in noble form again and again in *In Memoriam:*

> Sweet human hand and lips and eye,
> Dear heavenly friend that canst not die;
>
> Strange friend, past, present, and to be;
> Loved deeplier, darklier understood;

Behold I dream a dream of good,
And mingle the world with thee.

Thy voice is on the rolling air;
I hear thee where the waters run;
Thou standest in the rising sun,
And in the setting thou art fair.

It is not loss, but momentary eclipse, and the final issue is a clearer perception of immortal love, and a deeper consciousness of eternal life.

The attitude, therefore, in any such bereavement — sore as the first stroke must be, since we are so much the creatures of habit, and it is hard to adjust ourselves to the new relationship — cannot be an attitude merely of resignation. That was the extent to which the imperfect revelation of the Old Testament brought men. They had to rest in their knowledge of God's faithfulness and goodness. The limit of their faith was "The Lord gave, and the Lord hath taken away."[46] But to resignation we can add joy: "Not dead, but sleepeth," said the Master of death and life to a sorrowing man.[47]

For one thing, it must mean the hallowing of memory. The eclipse of love makes the love fairer when the eclipse passes. The loss of the outward purifies the affection and softens the heart. It brings out into fact what was often only latent in feeling. Memory adds a tender glory to the past. We think of only the virtues of the dead; we forget their faults. This is as it should be. We rightly love the immortal part of them; the fire

[46] Job 1:21.
[47] Matt. 9:24; Mark 5:39; Luke 8:52.

has burned up the dross and left pure gold. If it is idealization, it represents that which will be, and that which really is.

We do not ask to forget; we do not want the so-called consolations that time brings. Such an insult to the past, as forgetfulness would be, means that we have not risen to the possibilities of communion of spirit afforded us in the present. We would rather that the wound should be ever fresh than that the image of the dear past should fade. It would be a loss to our best life if it would fade. There is no sting in such a faith. Such remembrance as this, which keeps the heart green, will not cumber the life. True sentiment does not weaken, but becomes an inspiration to make our life worthy of our love. It can save even a squalid lot from sordidness; for however poor we may be in the world's goods, we are rich in happy associations in the past, and in sweet communion in the present, and in blessed hope for the future.

Chapter Six

Guard against threats
to friendship

The eclipse of friendship through death is not nearly so sad as the many ways in which friendship may be wrecked. There are worse losses than the losses of death, and to bury a friendship is a keener grief than to bury a friend. The latter softens the heart and sweetens the life, while the former hardens and embitters.

The Persian poet Hafiz says, "Thou learnest no secret until thou knowest friendship; since to the unloving no heavenly knowledge enters." But so imperfect are our human relationships that many a person has felt that he has bought his knowledge too dearly. Few of us go through the world without some scars on the heart that still throb if the finger of memory touches them. In spite of all that has been said, and may be said, in praise of this golden friendship, it has been too often found how vain is the help of man. The deepest tragedies of life have been the failure of this very relationship.

In one way or another, the loss of friendship comes to all. The shores of life are strewn with wrecks. The convoy that left the harbor gaily in the sunshine cannot all expect to arrive together in the haven. There are the danger of storms and collisions, the separation of the night, and even at the best, if accidents never occur, the whole company cannot all keep up with the speed of the swiftest.

The Art of Being a Good Friend

There is a certain pathos in all loss, but there is not always pain in it, or at least it is of varied quality and extent. Some losses are natural and unavoidable, quite beyond our control, the result of resistless change. Some loss is even the necessary accompaniment of gain. The loss of youth with all its possessions is the gain of manhood and womanhood. A person must put away childish things, the speech and understanding and thought of a child.[48] So the loss of some friendship comes as a part of the natural course of things and is accepted without mutilating the life.

Many of our connections with people are admittedly casual and temporary. They exist for mutual convenience through common interest at the time, or common purpose, or common business. None of the partners asks for more than the advantage each derives from the connection. When it comes to an end, we let the cable slip easily and say goodbye with a cheery wave. With many people, we meet and part in all friendliness and good feeling, and will be glad to meet again, but the parting does not tear our affections by the roots. When the business is transacted, the tie is loosened, and we go our separate ways without much regret.

At other times, there is no thought of gain, except the mutual advantage of conversation or companionship. We are pleasant to each other and enjoy the interchange of kindred tastes. Most of us have some pleasant recollections of happy meetings with interesting people, when we felt we would be glad to see them again if fortune turned around the wheel again to the same place; but, even though it hardly ever came

[48] Cf. 1 Cor. 13:11.

about that an opportunity of meeting occurred, we do not feel that our life is much the poorer for the loss.

◎

You can grow out of friendship

Also, we *grow* out of some of our friendships. This is to be expected, since so many of them were formed thoughtlessly or before we really knew either ourselves or our friends. They never meant very much to us. Most childhood friendships as a rule do not last long, because they are not based on the qualities that wear well. The comradeships of schoolchildren are usually due to propinquity rather than to character. They are the fruit of accident rather than of affinity of soul. Children grow out of these as they grow out of their clothes. Now and again, they suffer from growing pains, but it is more discomfort than anything else.

It is sad to look back and realize how few of one's early companionships remain, but it is not possible to blame either party for the loss. Distance, separation of interest, difference of work: all operate to divide. When athletics seemed the end of existence, friendship was based on football and baseball. But as life opens out, other standards are set up, and a new principle of selection takes its place. When the world is seen to be more than a ballground, when it is recognized to be a stage on which people play many parts, a new sort of intimacy is demanded, and it does not follow that it will be with the same persons. Such loss as this is the condition that accompanies the gain of growth.

◎

Some friendships die of neglect

There is more chance for the permanence of friendships formed a little later. It must not be too long after this period, however, for, when the generous time of youth has wholly passed, it becomes hard to make new connections. Men get overburdened with cares and personal concerns, and grow cautious about making advances. In youth, the heart is responsive and ready to be generous, the hand aches for the grasp of a comrade's hand, and the mind demands fellowship in the great thoughts that are beginning to dawn upon it. The closest friendships are formed early in life, just because then we are less cautious, more open to impressions, and readier to welcome self-revelations. After middle life, a person does not find it easy to give himself away and keeps a firmer hand on his feelings. Whatever are the faults of youth, it is unworldly in its estimates as a rule, and uncalculating in its thoughts of the future.

The danger to such friendship is the danger of just letting it lapse. As life spreads out before the eager feet, new interests crop up, new relations are formed, and the old tie gets worn away, from want of adding fresh strands to it. We may believe the advice about not forsaking an old friend because the new is not comparable to him, but we can neglect it by merely letting slip past things that, if used, would be a new bond of union.

As it is easier for some temperaments to make friends, it is easier for some dispositions to keep them. Little faults of manner, little occasions of thoughtlessness, or lack of the little courtesies do more to separate people than glaring mistakes do. There are some people so built that it is difficult to remain on very close terms with them; there are so many corners to knock against. Even strength of character, if unmodified by sweetness of disposition, adds to the difficulty of pulling together. Strong will can so easily develop into self-will; decision can become dogmatism. Wit, the salt of conversation, loses its savor when it becomes ill-natured. A faculty for argument is in danger of being mere quarrelsomeness.

The ordinary amenities of life must be preserved among friends. We can never feel very safe with the person whose humor tends to bitter speaking or keen sarcasm, or with the one who flares up into hasty speech at every or no provocation, or with the one who is argumentative and assertive. There are more breaches of the peace among friends through sins of speech than from any other cause. We do not treat our friends with enough respect. We make the vulgar mistake of looking upon the common as if it were therefore cheap in nature. We ought rather to treat our friend with a sort of sacred familiarity, as if we appreciated the precious gift his friendship is.

Every change in a person's life brings a risk of letting go something of the past with which it is a loss to part. A change of work, or a change of residence, or entrance into a larger sphere brings a certain engrossment that leads to neglect of the richest relationships in the past life. To many, even marriage has had a drop of bitterness in it, because it has somehow meant the severing of old and sacred links. This may be due to preoccupation and a subtle form of selfishness. The fire needs to be kept alive with fuel. To preserve it, there must be forethought, care, and love expended as before.

Friendship may lapse through the *misfortune of distance*. Absence does not always make the heart grow fonder. It does so only when the heart is securely fixed and when it is a heart worth fixing. More often, the other proverb is truer: out of sight, out of mind. It is so easy for a person to become self-centered and to impoverish his affections through sheer neglect. Ties once close get frayed and strained until they break, and we discover that we have said farewell to the past. Some kind of connection is needed to maintain friendship. There is a pathos about this gradual drifting away of lives, borne from each other, it sometimes seems, by opposing tides, as if a resistless power separated them:

> And bade betwixt their souls to be
> The unplumbed, salt, estranging sea.[49]

Or friendship may lapse through the *fault of silence*. The misfortune of distance may be overcome by love, but the fault of silence crushes our feeling as the falling rain kills the kindling beacon. Even the estrangements and misunderstandings that arise to all could not long remain where there is a frank and candid interchange of thought. Hearts grow cold toward each other through neglect. There is a suggestive word from the old Scandinavian *Edda*: "Go often to the house of thy friend; for weeds soon choke up the unused path." It is hard to overcome again the alienation caused by neglect, for there grows up a sense of resentment and injured feeling.

‿

Money can ruin friendships

Among the petty things that wreck friendships, none is so common and so unworthy as money. It is pitiable that it should be so. Thackeray speaks of the remarkable way in which a five-pound note will break up a half century's attachment between two brethren, and it is a common cynical remark of the world that the way to lose a friend is to lend him money. There is

---

[49] Matthew Arnold, "To Marguerite — Continued."

nothing that seems to affect the mind, and color the very heart's blood, more than money. There seems a curse in it sometimes, so potent is it for mischief. Poverty, if it is too oppressive grinding down the face,[50] may often hurt the heart-life; but, perhaps more often still, it only reveals what true treasures there are in the wealth of the affections. Whereas, we know what heartburnings, rivalries, and envyings are occasioned by this golden apple of discord. Most of the disputes that separate brethren are about the dividing of the inheritance, and it does seem to be the case that few friendships can survive the test of money.

> Neither a borrower, nor a lender be
> For loan oft loses both itself and friend.[51]

There must be something wrong with the friendship that so breaks down. It ought to be able to stand a severer strain than that. But the inner reason for the failure is often that there has been a moral degeneracy going on, and a weakening of the fiber of character on one side, or on both sides. The particular dispute, whether it be about money or about anything else, is only the occasion that reveals the slackening of the morale. The innate delicacy and self-respect of the friend who asks the favor may have been damaged through a series of similar importunities, or there may have been a growing hardness of heart and selfishness in the friend who refuses the request. Otherwise, if two are on terms of communion, it is hard to see why the giving or receiving of this service should be any more

[50] Cf. Isa. 3:15.
[51] William Shakespeare, *Hamlet*, Act 1, scene 3.

unworthy than any other help that friends can grant to each other. True commerce of the heart should make all other needful commerce possible.

⁔

Selfishness and poor judgment can ruin friendship

Friendship has also been wrecked by outside means, by the evil of others, through the evil speaking, or the envy, or the whispering tongues that delight in scandal. Some mean natures rejoice in sowing discord, carrying tales with just the slightest turn of a phrase, or even a tone of the voice that gives a sinister reading to an innocent word or act. Frankness can always prevent such from permanently wrecking friendship.

Besides, we should judge no one, still less a trusted friend, by a report of an incident or a hasty word. We should judge our friend by his record, by what we know of his character. When anything inconsistent with that character comes before our notice, it is only justice to him at least to suspend judgment, and it would be wisdom to refuse to credit it at all.

We sometimes wonder to find a friend cold and distant to us, and perhaps we moralize on man's fickleness and inconstancy, but the reason may be to seek in ourselves. We cannot expect the pleasure of friendship without the duty, the privilege without the responsibility. We cannot break off the threads of the web, and then, when the mood is on us, continue it as though nothing had happened. If such a breakage has occurred, we must go back and patiently join the threads together again.

Thoughtlessness has done more harm in this respect than has ill will. If we have lost a friend through selfish neglect, the loss is ours, and we cannot expect to take up the story where we left off years ago. There is a serene impudence about the treatment some mete out to their friends, dropping their friends whenever it suits them and thinking to take them up when it once more happens to suit them. We cannot expect to walk with another when we have gone for miles along another way. We will have to go back and catch him up again. If the fault has been ours, desire and shame will give our feet wings.

⁓

Spiritual union is necessary for friendship

The real source of separation is ultimately a spiritual one. We cannot walk with another unless we are agreed.[52] The lapse of friendship is often due to this: that one has let the other travel on alone. If one has sought pleasure, and the other has sought truth; if one has cumbered his life with the trivial and the petty, and the other has filled his with high thoughts and noble aspirations; if their hearts are on different levels, it is natural that they should now be apart. We cannot stay behind with the camp followers and, at the same time, fight in the vanguard with the heroes. If we wish to keep our best friends, we must go with them in sympathy, and be able to share their thoughts.

In the letters of Dean Stanley, there is one from Jowett to Stanley that brings out this necessity: "I earnestly hope that the friendship, which commenced between us many years ago, may be a blessing to last us through life. I feel that if it is to be so, we must both go onward, otherwise the tear and wear of life, and the 'having traveled over each other's minds,' and a thousand accidents will be sufficient to break it off. I have

[52] Cf. Amos 3:3.

often felt the inability to converse with you, but never for an instant the least alienation. There is no one who would not think me happy in having such a friend."

It is not, however, so much the equal pace of the mind that is necessary as the equal pace of the spirit. We may think about a very brilliant friend that he will outstrip us and outgrow us. The fear is natural, but if there is spiritual oneness, it is an unfounded fear.

> Yet oft, when sundown skirts the moor,
> An inner trouble I behold,
> A spectral doubt which makes me cold,
> That I should be thy mate no more.

But love is not dependent on intellect. The great bond of union is not that both parties are alike in mind, but that they are akin in soul. Mere intellect only divides men further than the ordinary natural and artificial distinctions that already exist. There are endless instances of this disuniting influence to be seen, in the contempt of learning for ignorance, the derisive attitude that knowledge assumes toward simplicity, the metropolitan disdain for provincial Galilee.[53]

It is love, not logic, that can unite people. Love is the one solvent to break down all barriers, and love has other grounds for its existence than merely intellectual ones. So, although similarity of taste is another bond and is perhaps necessary for the perfect friendship, it is not its foundation; and if the foundation is not undermined, there is no reason why difference of mental power should wreck the structure.

[53] Cf. John 7:41.

However it happen that friends are separated, it is always sad, for the loss of a friendship is the loss of an ideal. Sadder than the pathos of unmated heart is the pathos of severed souls. It is always a pain to find a friend look on us with cold stranger's eyes and to know ourselves dead of hopes of future closeness. It is a pain even when we have nothing to blame ourselves with, but much more so when we feel that ours is the fault.

It would not seem to matter very much, if it were not such a loss to both, for friendship is one of the appointed means of saving the life from worldliness and selfishness. It is the greatest education in the world, for it is education of the whole person — of the affections as well as the intellect. Nothing of worldly success can make up for the want of it. And true friendship is also a moral preservative. It teaches something of the joy of service and the beauty of sacrifice. We cannot live an utterly useless life if we have to think for, and act for, another. It keeps love in the heart and keeps God in the life.

Faithlessness is the greatest destroyer of friendship

The greatest and most irretrievable wreck of friendship is the result of a moral breakdown in one of the associates. Worse than the separation of the grave is the desolation of the heart by faithlessness. More impassable than the gulf of distance with the estranging sea, more separating than the gulf of death, is the great gulf fixed between souls through deceit and shame. Said a sorrowful psalmist who had known this experience, "Mine own familiar friend in whom I trusted, which did eat of my bread, hath lifted up his heel against me."[54] And another

---

[54] Ps. 41:9.

psalmist sobs the same lament: "It was not an enemy that reproached me; then I could have borne it; . . . but it was thou, a man mine equal, my guide and mine acquaintance. We took sweet counsel together, and walked into the house of God in company."[55] The loss of a friend by any of the common means is not so hard as to find a friend faithless. The trustful soul has often been disillusioned thus. The rod has broken in the hand that leaned on it and has left its red wound on the palm. There is a deeper wound on the heart.

The result of such a breakdown of comradeship is often bitterness and cynical distrust of man. It is this experience that gives point to the worldling's sneer: "Defend me from my friends; I can defend myself from my enemies." We cannot wonder sometimes at the cynicism. It is like treason within the camp, against which no one can guard. It is a stab in the back, a cowardly assassination of the heart. Treachery like this usually means a sudden fall from the ideal for the deceived one, and the ideal can be recovered only, if at all, by a slow and toilsome ascent, foot by foot and step by step.

Failure of one often leads to distrust of all. This is the terrible responsibility of friendship. We have more than the happiness of our friend in our power; we have his faith. Most men who are cynical about women are so because of the inconstancy of one. Most sneers at friendship are, to begin with at least, the expression of individual pain, because the person has known the shock of the lifted heel. Distrust works havoc on the character, for it ends in unbelief of goodness itself. And distrust always meets with its own likeness and is paid back in

[55] Ps. 55:12-14.

its own coin. Suspicion breeds suspicion, and the conduct of life on such principles becomes a tug-of-war.

The social virtues, which keep the whole community together, are thus closely allied to the supreme virtue of friendship. Aristotle had reason in making it the nexus between his *Ethics* and his *Politics*. Truth, good faith, and honest dealing between one person and another are necessary for any kind of relationship, even that of business. People can do nothing with each other if they have not a certain minimum of trust. There have been times when there seems to be almost an epidemic of faithlessness, when the social bond seems loosened, when people's hands are raised against each other, when confidence is paralyzed, and people hardly know whom to trust.

The prophet Micah, who lived in such a time, expresses this state of distrust: "Trust ye not any friend, put ye no confidence in a familiar friend. A man's enemies are of his own household."[56] This means anarchy, and society becomes like a bundle of sticks with the cord cut. The cause is always a decay of religion, for law is based on morality, and morality finds its strongest sanction in religion. Selfishness results in anarchy.

The story of the French Revolution has in it some of the darkest pages in the history of modern civilization, due to the breakdown of social trust. The revolution took to devouring her own children. Suspicion, during the reign of terror, brooded over the heads of men and oppressed their hearts. The ties of blood and fellowship seemed broken, and the sad words of Christ had their horrid fulfillment, that the brother would deliver up the brother to death, and "the father the child, and

[56] Mic. 7:6.

the children rise up against their parents and cause them to be put to death."[57]

There are some awful possibilities in human nature. In Paris of those days, one had to be ever on his guard, to watch his acts, his words, even his looks. It meant for a time a collapse of the whole idea of the state. It was a panic, worse than avowed civil war. Friendship, of course, could have little place in such a frightful palsy of mutual confidence, although there were, for the honor of the race, some noble exceptions. The wreck of friendship through deceit is always a step toward social anarchy, for it helps to break down trust and good faith among men.

The wreck of friendship is also a blow to religion. Many have lost their faith in God, because they have lost, through faithlessness, their faith in man. Doubt of the reality of love becomes doubt of the reality of the spiritual life. To be unable to see the divine in man is to have the eyes blinded to the divine anywhere. Deception in the sphere of love shakes the foundation of religion. Its result is atheism, not perhaps as a conscious speculative system of thought, but as a subtle practical influence on conduct. It corrupts the fountain of life and taints the whole stream. Despair of love, if final and complete, would be despair of God, for God is love. Thus, the wreck of friendship often means a temporary wreck of faith. It ought not to be so, but that there is a danger of it should impress us with a deeper sense of the responsibility attached to our friendships. Our life follows the fortunes of our love.

[57] Cf. Matt. 10:21.

Chapter Seven

Take the initiative in renewing your friendships

It is a sentiment of the poets and romancers that love is rather helped by quarrels. There must be some truth in it, since we find the idea expressed a hundred times in different forms in literature. We find it among the wisdom of the ancients, and it remains one of the conventional properties of the dramatist and one of the accepted traditions of the novelist. It is expressed in maxim and apothegm, in play and poem. One of our old pre-Elizabethan writers has put it in classic form in English: "The falling out of faithful friends is the renewing of love."[58]

It is the chief stock-in-trade of the writer of fiction to depict the misunderstandings that arise between two persons through the sin of one, or the folly of both, or the villainy of a third; then come the means by which the tangled skein is unraveled, and in the end everything is satisfactorily explained, and the sorely tried characters are ushered into a happiness stronger and sweeter than ever before. Friends quarrel and are miserable in their state of separation; and, afterward, when the friendship is renewed, it is discovered that the bitter dispute was only a blessing in disguise, as the renewal itself was an

[58] Cf. Richard Edwards, *The Paradise of Dainty Devices*, "Amantium Irae."

exquisite pleasure, and the result has been a firmer and more stable relationship of love and trust.

The truth in this sentiment is, of course, the evident one, that a person often only wakens to the value of a possession when he is in danger of losing it. The force of a current is sometimes only noted when it is opposed by an obstacle.

Two persons may discover, by a temporary alienation, how much they really care for each other. It may be that previously they took things for granted. Their affection had lost its first glitter and was accepted as a commonplace. Through some misunderstanding or dispute, they broke off their friendly relationship, feeling sure that they had come to an end of their regard. They could never again be on the same close terms; hot words had been spoken; taunts and reproaches had passed; eyes had flashed fire; and they parted in anger — only to learn that their love for each other was as real and as strong as ever. The very difference revealed the true union of hearts that had existed. They had been blind to the strength of their mutual regard, until it was so painfully brought to their notice. The love is renewed with a more tender sense of its sacredness and a more profound feeling of its strength. The dissensions only displayed the union; the discord drove them to a fuller harmony. This is a natural and common experience.

⌒

Dissension endangers friendship
But a mistake may easily be made by confusing cause and effect. "The course of true love never did run smooth,"[59] but

---

[59] William Shakespeare, A *Midsummer Night's Dream*, Act 1, scene 1.

the obstacles in the channel do not *produce* the swiftness and the volume of the stream; they only *show* them. There may be an unsuspected depth and force for the first time brought to light when the stream strikes a barrier, but the barrier is merely the occasion, not the cause, of the revelation. To mistake the one for the other may lead to a false and stupid policy. Many, through this mistake, act as if dissension were of the very nature of affection, and as if the one must necessarily react on the other for good. Some foolish people will sometimes even produce disagreement for the supposed pleasure of agreeing once more, and quarrel for the sake of making it up again.

Rather, the end of love is near at hand when wrangling can live in its presence. It is not true that love is helped by quarrels, except in the small sense already indicated. A person may quarrel once too often with his friend, and a brother offended, says the proverb, is harder to be won than a strong city, and such contentions are like the bars of a castle.

It is always a dangerous experiment — besides being often a cruel one — willfully to test affection. Disputing is a shock to confidence, and without confidence, friendship cannot continue. A state of feud, even if a temporary one, often embitters the life and leaves its mark on the heart. Desolated homes and lonely lives are witnesses of the folly of any such policy. From the root of bitterness, there cannot possibly blossom any of the fair flowers of love. The surface truth of the poets' sentiment we have acknowledged and accounted for, but it is only a surface truth.

The best of friends will fall out, and the best of them will renew their friendship, but it is always at a great risk, and sometimes it strains the foundations of their esteem for each other to shaking:

> And blessings on the falling out
> That all the more endears,
> When we fall out with those we love
> And kiss again with tears![60]

But in any serious rupture of friendship, it can be only a blessing when it means the tears of repentance, and these are often tears of blood. In all renewing, there must be an element of repentance, and however great the joy of having regained the old footing, there is the memory of pain and the presence of regret. To cultivate contention as an art, and to trade upon the supposed benefit of renewing friendship, is a folly that brings its own retribution. The disputatious person for this reason never makes a good friend. In friendship people look for peace, concord, and some measure of content. There are enough battles to fight outside, enough jarring and jostling in the street, enough disputing in the marketplace, enough discord in the workaday world, without having to look for contention in the realm of the inner life also. There, if anywhere, we ask for an end of strife. Friendship is the sanctuary of the heart, and the peace of the sanctuary should hover over it. Its chief glory is that the dust and noise of contest are excluded.

⌒

Offenses from loved ones are the most painful
It must be that offenses come. It is not only that the world is full of conflict and controversy, and everyone must take his

[60] Alfred, Lord Tennyson, *The Princess*, Part 2.

share in the fights of his time. We are born into the battle; we are born for the battle. But apart from the outside strife, from which we cannot separate ourselves, and should not desire to separate ourselves, the strange thing is that it looks as if it must be that offenses come even among brethren.

The bitterest disputes in life are among those who are nearest each other in spirit. We do not quarrel with the man in the street, the man with whom we have little or no communication. He has not the chance, nor the power, to chafe our soul and ruffle our temper. If need be, we can afford to despise, or at least to neglect, him. It is one of our own household, near us in life and spirit, who runs the risk of the only serious dissensions with us. One with whom we have most points of contact presents the greatest number of places where difference can occur. Only from circles that touch each other can a tangent strike off from the same point.

A person can make enemies only among his friends. A certain amount of opposition and enmity a person must be prepared for in this world, unless he lives a very invertebrate life. Outside opposition cannot embitter, for it cannot touch the soul. But that two who have walked as friends, one in aim and one in heart, perhaps of the same household of Faith, should stand face-to-face with hard brows and gleaming eyes, should speak as foes and not as lovers of the same love, is, in spite of the poets and romancers, the bitterest moment of life.

There are some we cannot hurt even if we would, whom all the venom of our nature could not touch, because we mean nothing to them. But there are others in our power whom we can stab with a word, and these are our brethren, our familiar friends, our comrades at work, our close associates, our fellow laborers in God's vineyard. It is not the crowd that idly jostles us in the street who can hurt us to the quick, but a familiar friend in whom we trusted. He has a means of ingress barred to strangers and can strike home as no other can. This is why family quarrels, ruptures in the inner circle, and Church disputes are so bitter. They come so near us. An offended brother is hard to win, because the very closeness of the previous intimacy brings a rankling sense of injustice and the resentment of injured love. An injury from the hand of a friend seems such a wanton thing, and the heart hardens itself with the sense of wrong, and a separation ensues like the bars of a castle.

It must be that offenses come, but woe unto him by whom they come.[61] The strife-makers find in themselves, in their barren hearts and empty lives, their own appropriate curse. The blow they strike comes back upon them. Worse than the choleric temperament is the peevish, sullen nature. The one usually finds a speedy repentance for his hot and hasty mood; the other is a constant menace to friendship and acts like a perpetual irritant. The root of this temperament is selfishness, and it grows by what it feeds on.

~

You should seek reconciliation after an offense

When offenses do come, we may indeed use them as opportunities for growth in gracious ways, and thus turn them into blessings on the lives of both. To the offended, it may be an occasion for patience and forgiveness; to the offender, an occasion for humility and frank confession; and to both, a renewing of love less open to offense in the future.

---

[61] Cf. Luke 17:1.

There are some general counsels about the making up of differences, although each case needs special treatment for itself, which will easily be found if once the desire for concord is established. Christ's recipe for a quarrel among brethren is "If thy brother shall trespass against thee, go and tell him his fault between thee and him alone; if he shall hear thee, thou hast gained thy brother."[62]

Much of our dissension is due to misunderstanding that could be put right by a few honest words and a little open dealing. Human beings so often live at cross purposes with each other, when a frank word or a simple confession of wrong, almost a look or a gesture, would heal the division. Resentment grows through brooding over a fancied slight. Hearts harden themselves in silence, and, as time goes on, it becomes more difficult to break through the silence. Through our sinful separations, our selfish exclusiveness, and our resentful pride, there is a terrible waste of human friendship, a waste of power that might be used to bless all our lives. We let the sweetest souls we have met die without acknowledging our debt to them. We stand aside in haughty isolation until the open grave opens our sealed hearts — too late. We let the chance of reconciliation pass until it is irrevocable. And in some cases, as with the friends in Coleridge's great poem, the parting has been eternal, and neither has ever since found another such friend to fill the life with comfort and free the hollow heart from paining.

There is more evil from such a state of discord than the mere loss it is to both; it influences the whole heart-life,

[62] Matt. 18:15.

creating sometimes bitterness, sometimes universal suspicion, and sometimes cynicism. Hatred is contagious, as love is. They have an effect on the whole character and are not confined to the single incident that causes the love or the hate. To hate a single one of God's creatures is to harden the heart to some extent against all. Love is the center of a circle that broadens out in ever-widening circumference.

Dante tells us in *La Vita Nuova* that the effect of his love for Beatrice was to open his heart to all and to sweeten all his life. He speaks of the surpassing virtue of her very salutation to him in the street. "When she appeared in any place, it seemed to me, by the hope of her excellent salutation, that there was no man mine enemy any longer; and such warmth of charity came upon me that most certainly in that moment I would have pardoned whomsoever had done me an injury; and if anyone should then have questioned me concerning any matter, I could only have said unto him 'Love,' with a countenance clothed in humbleness." His love bred sweetness in his mind and took in everything within the blessed sweep of its range.

Hatred also is the center of a circle, which has a baneful effect on the whole life. We cannot have bitterness or resentment in our mind without its coloring every thought and affection. Hatred of one will affect our attitude toward all.

⌒

Reconciliation calls for considerateness

If, then, we possess the spirit to be reconciled with an offended or an offending brother, there are some things that may be said about the tactics of renewing the broken tie. There is needed a certain tactful considerateness. In all such questions, the grace of the act depends as much on the *manner* of it as on the act itself. The grace of the fairest act may be hurt by a boorish blemish of manner. Many a graceful act is spoiled by a graceless touch, as a generous deed can be ruined by a grudging manner. An air of condescension will destroy the value of the finest charity. There is a forgiveness that is no forgiveness — formal, constrained, from the teeth and lips outward. It does not come as the warm breath that has had contact with the blood of the heart. The highest forgiveness is so full and free that it is forgetfulness. It is complete as the forgiveness of God.

If there is something in the method of the approach, there is perhaps more in the time of it. It ought to be chosen carefully and considerately; for it may be that the other has not been prepared for the renewal by thought and feeling, as the one who makes the advances has been.

No hard and fast rule can be formulated when dealing with such a complex and varied subject as man. So much depends on temper and character. One person taken by surprise reveals his true feeling; another, when taken off his guard, is irritated and shuts up his heart in a sort of instinctive self-defense.

The thoughtfulness of love will suggest the appropriate means, but some emphasis may rightly be given to the phrase in Christ's counsel: "between thee and him alone." Let there be an opportunity for a frank and private conversation. To appeal to an estranged friend in front of witnesses induces to special pleading, making the witnesses the jury, asking for a verdict on either side. And the result is that both are still convinced that they have right on their side and that they have been wronged.

The Art of Being a Good Friend

～

Do not hesitate to reconcile with your friend

If the fault of the estrangement lies with us, the burden of confession should rest upon us also. To go to our friend with sincere penitence is no more than our duty. Whether the result is successful or not, it will mean a blessing for our own soul. Humility brings its own reward, for it brings God into one's life. Even if we have cause to suspect that the offended brother will not receive us kindly, still such reparation as we can make is at least the gate to reconciliation. It may be too late, but confession will lighten the burden on our own heart. Our brother may be so offended that he is harder to be won than a strong city, but he is far more worth winning; and even if the effort is unsuccessful, it is better than the cowardice that suffers a bloodless defeat.

If, on the other hand, the fault was not ours, our duty is still clear. It should be even easier to take the initiative in such a case; for after all, it is much easier to forgive than to submit to be forgiven. To some natures, it is hard to be laid under an obligation, and the generosity of love must be shown by the offended brother. He must show the other his fault gently and generously, not parading his forgiveness like a virtue, but as if the favor were on his side — as it is.

Christ made forgiveness the test of spirituality. If we do not know the grace of forgiveness, we do not know how gracious life may be. The highest happiness is not a matter of possessions and material gains, but has its source in a heart at peace; and thus it is that the renewing of friendship has a spiritual result. If we are revengeful, censorious, judging others harshly, always putting the worst construction on a word or an act, uncharitable, or unforgiving, we certainly cannot claim kin-ship with the spirit of the Lord Jesus. St. Paul made the opposite the very test of the spiritual person: "Brethren, if a man be overtaken in a fault, ye which are spiritual restore such a one in the spirit of meekness."[63]

If we knew all, we would forgive all. If we knew all the facts, the things that produced the petulance, the soreness that caused the irritation, we would be ready to pardon, for we would understand the temptation. If we knew all, our hearts would be full of compassionate love even for those who have wronged us. They have wronged themselves more than they can possibly wrong us; they have wounded a person to their own hurt.

⤻

Reconciliation brings you Christ's peace

To think kindly once more of a separated friend, to soften the heart toward an offending brother, will bring the blessing of the Peacemaker, the blessing of the Reconciler. The way to be sure of acting this part is to pray for the friend. We cannot remain angry with another when we pray for him. Offense departs when prayer comes. The captivity of Job was turned when he prayed for his friends.

If we stubbornly refuse the renewing of friendship, it is an offense against religion also. Only love can fulfill the law of Christ. His is the Gospel of reconciliation, and the greater reconciliation includes the lesser. The friends of Christ must be friends of one another. That ought to be accepted as an axiom. To be reconciled to God carries with it at least a disposition of

---

[63] Gal. 6:1.

heart that makes it easy to be reconciled to others also. We have cause to suspect our religion if it does not make us gentle, forbearing, and forgiving — if the love of our Lord does not so flood our hearts as to cleanse them of all bitterness, spite, and wrath. If a person is nursing anger, if he is letting his mind become a nest of foul passions, malice, and hatred, and evil wishing, how can the love of God dwell in him?

If we cannot, at need, even humiliate ourselves to win our brother, it is difficult to see where our religion comes in, especially when we think what humiliation Christ suffered so that He might reconcile us to God, and make us friends again with our heavenly Father, and renew our broken love. Whatever our faith and works may be, and however correct our creed and conduct, if we give place to anger, if we stiffen ourselves in strife and disdain, we are none of His, who was meek and lowly of heart. We may come to the sanctuary with lips full of praises and eyes full of prayers, with devotion in our hearts and gifts in our hand, but God will spurn our worship and despise our gifts.

It is not a small matter, this renewing of friendship, but it is the root of religion itself and is well made the very test of spiritual-mindedness. "If thou bring thy gift to the altar, and there rememberest that thy brother hath aught against thee, leave there thy gift before the altar, and go thy way; first be reconciled to thy brother, and then come and offer thy gift."[64] Misunderstandings and estrangements will arise, occasions will come when it seems as if not even love and forbearance can avoid a quarrel, but surely Christ has died in vain if His grace cannot save us from the continuance of strife.

[64] Matt. 5:23-24.

Such renewing of love, done with this high motive, will indeed bring an added joy, as the poets have declared. The very pain will give zest to the pleasure. We will take the great gift of friendship with a new sense of its beauty and sacredness. We will walk more softly because of the experience, and more than ever will tremble lest we lose it. For days after the reconciliation, we will go about with the feeling that the benediction of the peacemakers rests on our head and clings around our feet.

But more than any personal joy from the renewed friendship, we will have the smile of God on our life. We will know that we have done what is well pleasing in His sight. Sweeter than the peace that comes from being at one with others is the peace that comes from being at one with God. It settles on the soul like the mist on the mountains, enveloping and enswathing it. It comes to our fevered life as a great calm. Over the broken waters there hovers the golden glory of God's eternal peace.

And more even than all that, we will have gained a new insight into the love of the Father and into the sacrifice of the Son. We will understand a little more of the mystery of the Love that became poor, that gladly went into the wilderness to seek and to save the lost.[65] The Cross will gain new and rich significance to us, and all the world will be an arena in which is enacted the spectacle of God's great love. The world is bathed in the love of God, as it is flooded by the blessed sun. If we are in the light and walk in love, our walk will be with God, and His gentleness will make us great.

[65] Cf. Luke 19:10.

The Art of Being a Good Friend

There is intended an ever fuller education in the meaning and in the life of love, until the assurance reaches us that nothing can separate us from love. Even death, which sunders us from our friends, cannot permanently divide us. In the great homecoming and reunion of hearts, all the veils that obscure feeling will be torn down, and we shall know each other better and shall love each other better.

Chapter Eight

*Respect the limits
of friendship*

Friendship, at its very best and purest, has limits. At its beginning, it seems to have no conditions and to be capable of endless development. In the first flush of newborn love, it seems almost an insult to question its absolute power to meet every demand made upon it. The exquisite joy of understanding, and being understood, is too keen to let us believe that there may be a terminal line beyond which we may not pass. Friendship comes as a mystery, formless, undefined, without set bounds; and it is often a sore experience to discover that it is circumscribed, and limited like everything human. At first, to speak of it as having qualifications was a profanation, and to find them out came as a disillusionment.

Yet the discovery is not all a loss. The limitless is also the vague, and it is good to know the exact terms implied in a relationship. Of course, we learn through experience the restrictions on all intimacy, and, if we are wise, we learn to keep well within the margin; but many a disappointment might have been saved if we had understood the inherent limitations of the subject. These are the result of personality. Each partner is, after all, a distinct individual, with will, conscience, and life apart, with a personal responsibility that none can take from him, and with an individual bias of mind and heart that can never be left out of account.

The Art of Being a Good Friend

As is to be expected, some of the limits of friendship are not essential to the relationship, but are due to a *defect* in the relationship, perhaps an idiosyncrasy of character or a peculiarity of temper. Some of the limits are self-imposed and arise from mistake of folly. A friend may be too exacting and may make excessive demands that strain the bond to the breaking point. There is often a good deal of selfishness in the affection, which asks for absorption, and is jealous of other interests. Jealousy is usually the fruit, not of love, but of self-love.

Life is bigger than any relationship, and it covers more ground. The circles of life may intersect, and part of each may be common to the other, but there will be an area on both sides exclusive to each. And even if it were possible for the circles to be concentric, it could hardly be that the circumference of the two could be the same; one would be, almost without a doubt, of larger radius than the other. It is not identity that is the aim and the glory of friendship, but unity in the midst of difference. To strive at identity is to be certain of failure, and it deserves failure, for it is the outcome of selfishness. A person's friend is not his property, to be claimed as his exclusive possession. Jealousy is an ignoble vice, because it has its roots in egotism. It also destroys affection, since it is evidence of want of trust, and trust is essential to friendship.

⌒

Friendship has physical, mental, and spiritual limits
There are physical limits to friendship, if nothing else. There are material barriers to be surmounted before human beings really get into touch with each other, even in the slightest degree. The bodily organs, through which alone we can enter into communication, carry with them their own disabilities.

The senses are at the best limited in their range, and are ever exposed to error. Flesh stands in the way of a complete revelation of soul. Human feet cannot enter past the threshold of the soul's abode. The very means of self-revelation is a self-concealment. The medium by which alone we know darkens, if it does not distort, the object. Words obscure thought by the very process through which alone thought is possible for us, and the fleshly wrappings of the soul hide it at the same time that they make it visible.

And if there are physical limits to friendship, there are greater mental limits. The needs of living press on us and drive us into different currents of action. Our varied experience colors all our thought, and gives a special bias to our mind. There is a personal equation that must always be taken into account. This is the charm of friendship, but it is also a limitation. We do not travel over the same ground; we meet, but we also part. However great the sympathy, it is not possible completely to enter into another person's mind and look at a subject with his eyes.

Much of our impatience with each other, as well as most of our misunderstandings, are caused by this natural limitation. The lines along which our minds travel can, at the best, be asymptotic — approaching each other indefinitely near, but never quite coinciding.

The greatest limit of friendship, of which these others are but indications, is the spiritual fact of the separate personality of each human being. This is seen most absolutely in the sphere of morals. The ultimate standard for a person is his own individual conscience, and neither the constraint of affection, nor the authority of numbers, can atone for falseness there.

~

Conscience must always supersede friendship

One of the most forceful illustrations of this final position of all religion is to be found in this passage of terrific intensity from the book of Deuteronomy: "If thy brother, the son of thy mother, or thy son or thy daughter, or the wife of thy bosom, or thy friend which is as thine own soul, entice thee secretly, saying, 'Let us go and serve other gods' . . . thou shalt not consent unto him, nor hearken unto him . . . but thine hand shall be first upon him to put him to death, and afterward the hand of all the people . . . because he has sought to thrust thee away from the Lord thy God."[66] The form of the passage, of course, gets its coloring from the needs of the time and the temper of the age. The book of Deuteronomy is so sure that the law of God is necessary for the life of Israel, and that departure from it will mean national ruin, that it will shrink from nothing needed to preserve the truth. Its warnings against being led away to idolatry are very urgent and solemn. Every precaution must be taken; nothing must be allowed to seduce them from their allegiance — not the most sacred ties, nor the most solemn authority. No measure of repression can be too stern.

In that fierce time, it was natural that apostasy should be thought worthy of death, for apostasy from religion meant also treason to the nation; much more those who used their influence to seduce people to apostasy were to be condemned. The passage is introduced by the assertion that if even a prophet, a recognized servant of God, attesting his prophecy with signs and wonders, should solicit others to leave the worship of

[66] Deut. 13:6, 8-10.

Jehovah, in spite of his sacred character, and in spite of the seeming evidence of miracles, they must turn from him with loathing, and his doom should be death. And if the apostasy should have the weight of numbers and a whole city go astray, the same doom is theirs. If the tenderest relationship should tempt the soul away, if a brother, or son, or daughter, or wife, or friend should entice to apostasy, the same relentless judgment must be meted out.

The fact that this stern treatment is advocated in the book of Deuteronomy, which is full of the most tender consideration for all weak things, shows the need of the time. Deuteronomy has some of the most beautiful legislation in favor of slaves and little children and birds and domestic animals, some of it in advance of even our modern customs and practices, permeated as these are by Christian sentiment. And it is in this finely sensitive book that we find such strong assertion of the paramount importance of individual responsibility.

The influence of a friend or near relative is bound to be great. We are affected on every side, and at every moment, by the environment of other lives. There is a spiritual affinity, which is the closest and most powerful thing in the world, and yet, in the realm of morals, it has definite limits set to it. At best, it can go only a certain length and ought not to be allowed to go further than its legitimate bounds.

The writer of Deuteronomy appreciated to the full the power and attraction of the near human relationships. We see this from the way he describes them, adding an additional touch of fondness to each: "thy brother, the son of thy mother, the wife of thy bosom, thy friend who is as thine own soul." But it sets a limit to the place even such tender ties should be allowed to have. The most intimate of relatives, the most trusted of friends, must not be permitted to abrogate the place of conscience. Affection may be perverted into an instrument of evil. There is a higher moral law than even the law of friendship. The demands of friendship must not be allowed to interfere with the dictates of duty. The moral law should be obeyed not blindly, but because in obeying it we are choosing the better part for both, for as Frederick Robertson truly says, "The man who prefers his dearest friend to the call of duty will soon show that he prefers himself to his dearest friend." Such weak giving in to the supposed higher demand of friendship is only a form of selfishness.

Friendship is at times too exacting. It asks for too much — more than we have to give, more than we ever ought to give. There is a tyranny of love, making demands that can be granted only to the loss of both. Such tyranny is a perversion of the nature of love, which is to serve, not to rule. It would override conscience and break down the will. We cannot give up our personal duty, as we cannot give up our personal responsibility. That is how it is possible for Christ to say that if a man love father, or mother, or wife more than Him, he is not worthy of Him.[67] No human being can take the place of God to another life; it is an act of blasphemy to attempt it.

There is a love that is evil in its selfishness. Its very exclusive claim is a sign of its evil root. The rights of the individual must not be renounced, even for love's sake. Human love can ask too much, and it asks too much when it would break down the individual will and conscience.

[67] Cf. Matt. 10:37.

> The hands that love us often are the hands
> That softly close our eyes and draw us earthward.
> We give them all the largesse of our life —
> Not this, not all the world, contenteth them,
> Till we renounce our rights as living souls.

We cannot renounce our rights as living souls without losing our souls. No one can pay the debt of life for us. No one can take the burden of life from us. To no one can we hand over the reins unreservedly. It would be cowardice, and cowardice is sin.

The first axiom of the spiritual life is the sacredness of the individuality of each person. We must respect each other's personality. Even when we have rights over other people, these rights are strictly limited and carry with them a corresponding duty to respect their rights also. The one intolerable despotism in the world is the attempt to put a yoke on the souls of men, and there are some forms of intimacy that approach that despotism. To transgress the moral bounds set to friendship is to make the highest forms of friendship impossible; for these are only reached when free spirits meet in the unity of the spirit.

The community of human life, of which we are learning much today, is a great fact. We are all bound up in the same bundle. In a very true sense, we stand or fall together. We are ever on our trial as a society — not only materially, but even in the highest things, morally and spiritually. There is a social conscience that we affect and that constantly affects us. We cannot rise very much above it; to fall much below it is for all true purposes to cease to live. We have recognized social standards that test morality; we have common ties, common duties, and common responsibilities.

⌒

Even the closest friendship
cannot reach a person's innermost self

But with it all, in spite of the fact of the community of human life, there is the other fact of the singleness of human life. We have a life that we must live *alone*. We can never get past the ultimate fact of the personal responsibility of each. We may be leaves from the same tree of life, but no two leaves are alike. We may be wrapped up in the same bundle, but one bundle can contain very different things. Each of us is colored with his own shade, separate and peculiar. We have our own special powers of intellect, our own special experience, our own moral conscience, our own moral life to live. So, while it is true that we stand or fall together, it is also true — and it is a deeper truth — that we stand or fall alone.

In this crowded world, with its interchanges and jostling, with its network of relationships, with its mingled web of life, we are each alone. Below the surface, there is a deep, and below the deep, there is a deeper depth. In the depth of the human heart, there is, and there must be, solitude. There is a limit to the possible communion with another. We never completely open up our nature to even our nearest and dearest. In spite of ourselves, something is kept back. It is not that we are untrue in this, and hide our inner self, but simply that we are unable to reveal ourselves entirely. There is a bitterness of the heart that only the heart knows; there is a joy of the heart with which no stranger can meddle; there is a boundary beyond which even a friend who is as our own soul becomes a stranger. There is a Holy of Holies,[68] over the threshold of which no human feet can pass. It is safe from trespass, guarded from intrusion, and even we cannot give to another the magic key to open the door.

In spite of all the complexity of our social life, and the endless connections we form with others, there is as the ultimate fact a great and almost weird solitude. We may fill up our hearts with human fellowship in all its grades, yet there remains to each a distinct and separated life.

We speak vaguely of the mass of people, but the mass consists of units, each with his own life, a thing apart. The community of human life is being emphasized today, and it is a lesson that bears and needs repetition, the lesson of our common ties and common duties. But at the same time, we dare not lose sight of the fact of the singleness of human life, if for no other reason than that otherwise we have no moral appeal to make on behalf of those ties and duties.

In the region of morals, in dealing with sin, we see how true this solitude is. There may be what we can truly call social and national sins, and persons can sin together, but, in its ultimate issue, sin is individual. It is a disintegrating thing, separating a person from his fellows, and separating him from God. We are alone with our sin, like the Ancient Mariner with the bodies of his messmates around him, each cursing him with his eye.[69]

---

[68] The Holy of Holies, the Temple's inner sanctuary, was entered only by the high priest on rare occasions; cf. Heb. 9:3 ff.

[69] Cf. Samuel Taylor Coledridge, "The Rime of the Ancient Mariner."

In the last issue, there is nothing in the universe but God and the single human soul. Others can share the sinning with us; no one can share the sin. "And the sin ye do by two and two, ye must pay for one by one."[70] Therefore, in this sphere of morals, there must be limits to friendship, even with the friend who is as our own soul.

⸙

Man's helplessness limits friendship

Friendship is a very real and close thing. It is one of the greatest joys in life and has noble fruits. We can do much for each other: there are burdens we can share; we can rejoice with those who do rejoice, and weep with those who weep.[71] Through sympathy and love, we are able to get out of self, and yet even here there are limits.

Our helplessness in the presence of grief, for instance, proves this fundamental singleness of human life. When we stand beside a friend before the open grave, under the cloud of a great sorrow, we learn how little we can do for him. We can only stand speechless, and pray that the great Comforter may come with His own divine tenderness, and enter the sanctuary of sorrow shut to feet of flesh. Mourners have indeed been soothed by a touch, or a look, or a prayer that had its source in a compassionate human heart, but it is only as a message of condolence flashed from one world to another.

There is a burden that everyone must bear, and none can bear for him, for there is a personality that, even if we would, we cannot unveil to human eyes. There are feelings sacred to

[70] Rudyard Kipling, "Tomlinson."
[71] Cf. Gal. 6:2; Rom. 12:15.

the person who feels. We have to "dree our own weird," and live our own life, and die our own death.

In the time of desolation, when the truth of this solitude is borne in on us, we are left to ourselves, not because our friends are unfeeling, but simply because they are unable. It is not their selfishness that keeps them off, but just their frailty. Their spirit may be willing, but the flesh is weak.[72] It is the lesson of life that there is no stay in the arm of flesh, that even if there is no limit to human love, there is a limit to human power. Sooner or later, somewhere or other, it is the experience of every son of man, as it was the experience of the Son of Man: "Behold, the hour cometh, and now is come, that ye, my friends, shall be scattered every man to his own, and shall leave me alone."[73]

Human friendship must have limits, just because it is human. It is subject to loss and is often to some extent the sport of occasion. It lacks permanence: misunderstandings can estrange us; slander can embitter us; death can bereave us. We are left very much the victims of circumstances, for, like everything earthly, friendship is open to change and decay. No matter how close and spiritual the friendship, it is not permanent and never certain. If nothing else, the shadow of death is always on it. Tennyson describes how he dreamed that he and his friend would pass through the world together, loving and trusting each other, and together pass out into the silence:

> Arrive at last the blessed goal,
> And He that died in Holy Land

[72] Cf. Matt. 26:41.
[73] Cf. John 16:32.

Would reach us out the shining hand,
And take us as a single soul.

It was a dream at the best. Neither to live together nor to die together could blot out the spiritual limits of friendship. Even in the closest of human relations, when two take each other for better, for worse, for richer, for poorer, in sickness and in health, they may be made one flesh, but never one soul. Singleness is the ultimate fact of human life. "The race is run by one and one, and never by two and two."

~

Friendship respects the personality of each individual

In religion, in the deepest things of the spirit, these limits we have been considering are perhaps felt most of all. With even a friend who is as one's own soul, we cannot seek to make a spiritual impression without realizing the constraint of his separate individuality. We cannot break through the barriers of another's distinct existence. If we have ever sought to lead to a higher life someone whom we love, we must have been made to feel that it does not all rest with us, that he is a free moral being, and that only by voluntarily yielding his heart and will and life to the King can he enter the Kingdom. We are forced to respect his personality. We may watch and pray and speak, but we cannot save.

There is almost a sort of spiritual indecency in unveiling the naked soul, in attempting to invade the personality of another life. There is sometimes a spiritual vivisection that some attempt in the name of religion, which is immoral. Only holier eyes than ours, only more reverent hands than ours, can deal with the spirit of a person. He is a separate individual, with all the rights of an individual. We may have many points of contact with him, the contact of mind on mind and heart on heart; we may even have rights over him, the rights of love; but he can at will insulate his life from ours. Here also, as elsewhere when we go deep enough into life, it is God and the single human soul.

The lesson of all true living in every sphere is to learn our own limitations. It is the first lesson in art to work within the essential limitations of the particular art. But in dealing with other lives, it is perhaps the hardest of all lessons to learn, and submit to, our limitations. It is the crowning grace of faith when we are willing to submit and to leave those we love in the hands of God, as we leave ourselves. Nowhere else is the limit of friendship so deeply cut as here in the things of the spirit.

> No man can save his brother's soul
> Nor pay his brother's debt.

Human friendship has limits because of the real greatness of man. We are too big to be quite comprehended by another. There is always something in us left unexplained and unexplored. We do not even know ourselves, much less can another hope to probe into the recesses of our being. Friendship has a limit, because of the infinite element in the soul. It is hard to be brought up by a limit along any line of life, but it is designed to send us to a deeper and richer development of our life. Man's limitation is God's occasion. Only God can fully satisfy the hungry heart of man.

Chapter Nine

Seek friendship with God

Life is an education in love. There are grades and steps in it, occasions of varying opportunity for the discipline of love. It comes to us at many points, trying us at different levels, so that it may get entrance somehow and so make our lives not altogether a failure. When we give up our selfishness and isolation, even in the most rudimentary degree, a beginning is made with us that is designed to carry us far, if we but follow the leading of our hearts.

There is an ideal toward which all our experience points. If it were not so, life would be a hopeless enigma and the world a meaningless farce. There must be a spiritual function intended, a design to build up strong and true moral character, to develop sweet and holy life; otherwise history is a despair, and experience a hopeless riddle. All truly great human life has been lived with a spiritual outlook and on a high level. People have felt instinctively that there is no justification for all the pain, strife, failure, and sorrow of the world if these do not serve a higher purpose than mere existence. Even our tenderest relationships need some more authoritative warrant than is to be found in them, even in the joy and hope they bring. That joy cannot be meant as an empty lure to keep life on the earth.

And the spiritual person has also discovered that the very breakdown of human ties leads to a larger and more permanent love. It is sooner or later found that the most perfect love cannot utterly satisfy the heart of man. All our human communion, blessed and helpful as it may be, must be necessarily fragmentary and partial. A person must discover that there is an infinite in him, which only the infinite can match and supply.

It is no disparagement of human friendship to admit this. It remains a blessed fact that it is possible to meet devotion that makes us both humble and proud: humble at the sight of its noble sacrifice; proud with a glad pride at its wondrous beauty. Man is capable of the highest heights of love. But man can never take the place of God, and, without God, life is shorn of its glory and divested of its meaning.

⌒

Human friendship reflects and leads to friendship with God

So the human heart has ever craved for a relationship deeper and more lasting than any possible among people — undisturbed by change, unmenaced by death, unbroken by fear, unclouded by doubt. The limitations and losses of earthly friendship are meant to drive us to the higher friendship. Life is an education in love, but the education is not complete until we learn the love of the eternal. Ordinary friendship has done its work when the limits of friendship are reached, when, through the discipline of love, we are led into a larger love, when a door is opened out to a higher life. The sickness of heart that is the lot of all, the loneliness that not even the voice of a friend can dispel, and the grief that seems to stop the pulse of life itself find their final meaning in this compulsion toward the divine. We are sometimes driven out not knowing whither we go, not knowing the purpose of it, but only knowing through sheer necessity that here we have no abiding city, or home, or life, or love, and seeking a city, a home, a life, a love that has foundations.

We have some training in the love of friends, as if only to prove to us that without love we cannot live. All our intimacies are but broken lights of the love of God. They are methods of preparation for the great communion. Insofar even that our earthly friendships are helps to life, it is because they are shot through with the spiritual, and they prepare us by their very deficiencies for something more permanent.

≈

Man's heart hungers for God

There have been implanted in man an instinct and a need that make him discontented until he finds content in God. If at any time we are forced to cease from man, whose breath is in his nostrils, it is that we may reach out to the infinite Father, unchanging, the same yesterday, today, and forever.[74] This is the clamant, imperious need of man.

The solitude of life in its ultimate issue is because we were made for a higher companionship. It is just in the innermost sanctuary, shut to every other visitant, that God meets us. We are driven to God by the needs of the heart. If the existence of God were due to a purely intellectual necessity, if we believed in Him only because our reason gave warrant for the faith, it would not matter much whether He really is and whether we really can know Him. But when the instincts of our nature and the necessities of the heart-life demand God, we are forced to

[74] Cf. Heb. 13:8.

believe. In moments of deep feeling, when all pretense is silenced, a person may be still able to question the *existence* of God, but he does not question his own *need* of God. Man, to remain man, must believe in the possibility of this relationship with the divine. There is a love that passeth all earthly love: the love of God to the weary, starved heart of man.

To believe in this great fact does not detract from human friendship, but, rather, really gives it worth and glory. It is because of this that all love has a place in the life of man. All our worships, friendships, and loves come from God and are but reflections of the divine tenderness. All that is beautiful, and lovely and pure, and of good repute finds its appropriate setting in God, for it was made by God. He made it for Himself.

He made man with instincts, aspirations, heart-hunger, and divine unrest, so that He might give them full satisfaction in Himself. He claims everything, but He gives everything. Our human relationships are sanctified and glorified by the spiritual union. He gives us back our kinships and friendships with a new light on them, an added tenderness, transfiguring our common ties and intimacies, flooding them with a supernal joy. We part from man to meet with God, so that we may be able to meet man again on a higher platform. But the love of God is the end and design of all other loves. If the flowers and leaves fade, it is because the time of ripe fruit is at hand. If these adornments are taken from the tree of life, it is to make room for the supreme fruitage.

Without the love of God, all other love would be but deception, luring men on to the awful disillusionment. We were born for the love of God; if we do not find it, it would be better for us if we had never been born.[75] We may have tasted of all the joys the world can offer, have known success and the gains of success, been blessed with the sweetest friendships and the most intense loves, but if we have not found love of God to be the chief end of life, we have missed our chance and can have at the last only a desolated life.

◌

God's friendship is enduring

But if, through the joy or through the sorrow of life, through love or the want of it, through the gaining of friends or the loss of them, we have been led to dower our lives with the friendship of God, we are possessed of the incorruptible and undefiled, and that does not pass away. The person who has it has attained the secret cheaply, even if it had to be purchased with his heart's blood, with the loss of his dream of blessedness. When the fabric of life crumbled to its native dust, and he rose out of its wreck, the vision of the eternal love came with the thrill of a great revelation. It was the entrance into the mystery, and the wonder of it awed him, and the joy of it inspired him, and he awakened to the fact that never again could he be *alone* to all eternity.

Communion with God is the great fact of life. All our forms of worship, all our ceremonies and symbols of religion, find their meaning here. There is, it is true, an ethic of religion, certain moral teachings valuable for life; there are truths of religion to be laid hold of by the reason; there are the consolations of religion to comfort the heart; but the root of all religion is this mystical union, a communion with the Unseen, a

[75] Cf. Matt. 26:24.

friendship with God open to man. Religion is not an acceptance of a creed, or a burden of commandments, but a personal secret of the soul, to be attained each person for himself. It is the experience of the nearness of God, the mysterious contact with the divine, and the consciousness that we stand in a special individual relationship with Him. The first state of exaltation, when the knowledge burst upon the soul, cannot, of course, last, but its effect remains in inward peace and outward impulse toward nobler life.

People of all ages have known this close relationship. The possibility of it is the glory of life: the fact of it is the romance of history and the true reading of history. All devout persons who have ever lived have lived in the light of this communion. All religious experience has had this in common, that somehow the soul is so possessed by God that doubt of His existence ceases; and the task of life becomes to keep step with Him, so that there may be correspondence between the outer and the inner conditions of life. People have known this communion in such a degree that they have been called preeminently the friends of God, but something of the experience that underlies the term is true of the pious persons of every generation.

To us, in our place in history, communion with God comes through Jesus Christ. It is an ineffable mystery, but it is still a fact of experience. Only through Jesus do we know God, His interest in us, His desire for us, and His purpose with us. He not only shows us in His own example the blessedness of a life in fellowship with the Father, but He makes it possible for us. United to Jesus, we know ourselves united to God. The power of Jesus is not limited to the historical impression made by His life. It entered the world as history; it lives in the world as spiritual fact today.

We offer Christ the submission of our hearts and the obedience of our lives, and He offers us His abiding presence. We take Him as our Master, and He takes us as His friends. "I call you no longer servants," He said to His disciples, "but I have called you friends."[76] The servant knows not what his Master does; his only duty is to obey. A friend is admitted to confidence, and although he may do the same thing as a servant, he does not do it any longer unreasoningly, but, having been taken into counsel, he knows why he is doing it. This was Christ's method with His disciples, not to apportion to each his task, but to show them His great purpose for the world, and to ask for their service and devotion to carry it out.

The distinction is not that a servant pleases his master, and a friend pleases himself. It is that our Lord takes us up into a relationship of love with Him, and we go out into life inspired with His spirit to work His work. It begins with the self-surrender of love, and love, not fear or favor, becomes the motive. To feel thus the touch of God on our lives changes the world. Its fruits are joy, and peace, and confidence that all the events of life are suffused, not only with meaning, but with a meaning of love. The higher friendship brings a satisfaction of the heart and a joy commensurate to the love. Its reward is itself, the sweet, enthralling relationship, not any adventitious gain it promises, either in the present, or for the future. Even if there were no physical, or moral, rewards and punishments in the world, we would still love and serve Christ *for His own*

[76] John 15:15.

sake. The soul that is bound by this personal attachment to Jesus has a life in the eternal, which transfigures the life in time with a great joy.

We can see at once that to be the friend of God means peace also. It has brought peace over the troubled lives of all His friends throughout the ages. Everyone who enters into the covenant knows the world to be a spiritual arena in which the love of God manifests itself. He walks no longer on a sodden earth and under a gray sky, for he knows that, although all people misunderstand him, he is understood, and followed with loving sympathy, in Heaven.

It was this confidence in God as a real and near friend that gave to Abraham's life such distinction, and the calm repose that made his character so impressive. Strong in the sense of God's friendship, he lived above the world, prodigal of present possessions, because sure of the future, waiting securely in the hope of the great salvation. He walked with God in sweet, unaffected piety and serene faith, letting his character ripen in the sunshine and living out his life as unto God, not unto men.

⎯

Friendship with God enhances human friendships

To know the love of God does not mean the impoverishing of our lives, by robbing them of their other sweet relations. Rather, it means the enriching of these by revealing their true beauty and purpose. Sometimes we are brought nearer to God through our friends, if not through their influence or the joy of their love, then through the discipline that comes from their very limitations and from their loss. But more often, the experience has been that, through our union with the Friend of friends, we are led into richer and fuller communion with our fellows. The nearer we get to the center of the circle, the nearer we get to each other. To be joined together in Christ is the only permanent union, deeper than the tie of blood, higher than the bond of kin, closer than the most sacred earthly relationship. Spiritual kinship is the great nexus to unite men. "Who are my brethren?" asked Jesus and, for an answer, pointed to His disciples and added, "Whosoever shall do the will of my Father in Heaven, the same is my mother and sister and brother."[77]

We ought to make more of our Christian friendships, the communion of the saints, the fellowship of believers. "They that feared the Lord spake often one to another,"[78] said the prophet Malachi in one of the darkest hours of the Church. What mutual comfort and renewed hope they would get from and give to each other! Faith can be increased, love stimulated, and enthusiasm revived by friendship.

The supreme friendship with Christ, therefore, will not take from us any of our treasured intimacies unless they are evil. It will increase the number of them and the true force of them. It will link us to all who love the same Lord in sincerity and truth. It will open our heart to the world of people whom Jesus loved and gave His life to save.

This friendship with the Lord knows no fear of loss; neither life, nor death, nor things present, nor things to come can separate us from it.[79] It is joy and strength in the present, and it

[77] Cf. Matt. 12:48, 50.
[78] Mal. 3:16.
[79] Cf. Rom. 8:38-39.

lights up the future with a great hope. We are not much concerned about speculations regarding the future, for we know we are in the hands of our Lover. All we care to assert of the future is that Christ will in an ever fuller degree be the environment of all Christian souls, and the effect of that constant environment will fulfill the aspiration of the apostle: "We shall be like Him, for we shall see Him as He is."[80] Communion produces likeness. Even now this is the test of our friendship with the Lord. Are we assimilating His mind, His way of looking at things, His judgments, His spirit? Is the Christ-conscience being developed in us? Have we an increasing interest in the things that interest Him, an increasing love of the things that He loves, an increasing desire to serve the purposes He has at heart? "Ye are my friends if ye do whatsoever I command you,"[81] is the test by which we can try ourselves.

Fellowship with Him, being much in His company, thinking of Him, and seeking to please Him will produce likeness and bring us together on more intimate terms. For, as love leads to the desire for fuller fellowship, so fellowship leads to a deeper love. Even if sometimes we almost doubt whether we are really in this blessed covenant of friendship, our policy is to go on loving Him, serving Him, and striving to please Him; and we will yet receive the assurance, which will bring peace. He will not disappoint us at the last. It is worth all the care and effort we can give to have and to keep for our friend Him who will be a lasting possession, whose life enters into the very fiber of our life, and whose love makes us certain of God.

[80] 1 John 3:2.
[81] John 15:14.

We ought to use our faith in this friendship to bless our lives. To have an earthly friend whom we trust and reverence can be to us a source of strength, keeping us from evil, making us ashamed of evil. The nearer the friend and the more spiritual the friendship, the keener is this feeling, and the more needful does it seem to maintain purity of heart.

⌒

Friendship with God can enrich the world profoundly
It must reach its height of intensity and of moral effectiveness in the case of friendship with God. There can be no motive on earth so powerful. If we could only have such a friendship, we see at once what an influence it might have over our life. We can appreciate more than the joy, peace, and comfort of it; we can feel the *power* of it. To know ourselves ever before a living, loving Presence, having a constant sense of Christ abiding in us, taking Him with us into the marketplace, into our business and our pleasure, to have Him as our familiar friend in joy and sorrow, in gain and loss, in success and failure, must, in accordance with all psychological law, be a source of strength, lifting life to a higher level of thought, feeling, and action.

Supposing it were true and possible, it would naturally be the strongest force in the world, the most effective motive that could be devised; it would affect the whole moral outlook and make easy some things now deemed impossible, and make impossible some things now, to our shame, too easy. Supposing this covenant with God were true, and we knew ourselves to have such a Lover of our soul, it would, as a matter of course, give us deeper and more serious views of human life, and yet take away from us the burden and the unrest of life.

Unless history is a lie, and experience a delusion, it is true. The world is vocal with a chorus of witness to the truth of it. From all sorts and conditions of people comes the testimony to its reality — from the old, who look forward to this Friend to make their bed in dying; from the young, who know His aid in the fiery furnace of temptation; from the strong, in the burden of the day and the dust of the battle, who know the rest of His love even in the sore labor; from the weak, who are mastered by His gracious compassion and inspired by His power to suffer and to bear. Christ's work on earth was to make the friendship of God possible to all. It seems too good to be true, too wondrous a condescension on His part, but its reality has been tested, and attested, by generations of believers. This covenant of friendship is open to us, to be ours in life, and in death, and past the gates of death.

The human means of communication is prayer, although we limit it sadly. Prayer is not an act of worship merely, the bending of the knee on set occasions, and offering petitions in need. It is an attitude of soul, opening the life on the Godward side and keeping free communication with the world of spirit. And so, it is possible to pray always, and to keep our friendship ever green and sweet; and God comes back upon the life, as dew upon the thirsty ground. There is an interchange of feeling, a responsiveness of love, a thrill of mutual friendship.

> You must love Him, ere to you
> He shall seem worthy of your love.

The great appeal of the Christian Faith is to Christian experience. Loving Christ is its own justification, as every loving heart knows. Life evidences itself; the existence of light is its own proof. The power of Christ on the heart needs no other argument than itself. People doubt only when the life has died out, and the light has waned, flickered, and spent itself. It is when there is no sign of the spirit in our midst, no token of forces beyond the normal and the usual, that we can deny the spirit. It is when faith is not in evidence that we can dispute faith. It is when love is dead that we can question love. The Christian Faith is not a creed, but a life; not a proposition, but a passion. Love is its own witness to the soul that loves; communion is its own attestation to the spirit that lives in the fellowship. The person who lives with Jesus knows Him to be a Lover who cleaves closer than a brother, a Friend who loves at all times, and a Brother born for adversity.

Friendship with Christ
springs from serving Him

It does not follow that there is an end of the question, so far as we are concerned, if we say that we at least do not know that friendship and cannot love Him. Some even say it with a wistful longing: "Oh, that I knew where I might find Him."[82] It is true that love cannot be forced, that it cannot be made to order, that we cannot love because we ought to, or even because we want to. But we can bring ourselves into the presence of the lovable. We can enter into friendship through the door of discipleship; we can learn love through service, and the day will come to us also when the Master's word will be true: "I call you no longer servant, but I call you friend."[83] His love

---

[82] Job 23:3.
[83] Cf. John 15:15.

will take possession of us until all else will seem as hatred in comparison.

To be called *friends* by our Master, to know Him as the Lover of our souls, to give Him entrance to our hearts, is to learn the meaning of living and to experience the ecstasy of living. The higher friendship is bestowed without money and without price, and is open to every heart responsive to God's great love.

> 'Tis only Heaven that is given away
> 'Tis only God may be had for the asking.

Biographical Note

Hugh Black
(1868-1953)

Born in Rothesay, Scotland, in 1868, Hugh Black graduated from Glasgow University in 1887. He spent his life in the service of God's people and gained fame as a pastor in Scotland and as a lecturer on homiletics in the United States. Even during his later service as a professor of theology, his pastoral vision remained warmly practical. Although he was not a Catholic, the common touch and engaging insights of his classic book *The Art of Being a Good Friend* shine forth for the benefit of Catholics and non-Catholics alike. He also wrote more than a dozen other books, including works on youth, work, and culture.

In *The Art of Being a Good Friend,* Black writes with keenness and sensitivity. He weaves Scripture, poetry, and his own lucid wisdom to reveal the deepest hungers of the heart of man and to show how those hungers can be fulfilled through friendship — with others and ultimately with God. His words show all Christians the critical elements that not only unite individual persons in deep, enduring friendship, but also lead to a deeper, more enduring love for God.